Chris Palmer doesn't just diagnose our meaning crisis, he leads us by the hand into Novemberton to see and experience the existential emptiness in the faces and lives of those who dwell there. With clarity and heart, he exposes the futility of life without God while offering a way back home to meaning, wonder, and the fullness of life found only in him. A must read for those who guide others toward meaning and for those still searching for it.

—Jana Harmon, PhD, author, *Atheists Finding God*; host, *eX-skeptic Podcast*

A fantastic guide to the practical power of worldview, this book shows how our views of God quietly shape how we live, choose, and endure in a tough world—whether with despair or with hope.

—Josh Rasmussen, Professor of Philosophy, Baylor University; author, *Who Are You, Really?*

A WORLD WITHOUT GOD

CHRIS PALMER

A WORLD WITHOUT GOD

The Search for Meaning in a Society Overwhelmed by Despair

ZONDERVAN REFLECTIVE

A World Without God

Published by Zondervan, 3950 Sparks Drive SE, Suite 101, Grand Rapids, MI 49546, USA. Zondervan is a registered trademark of The Zondervan Corporation, L.L.C., a wholly owned subsidiary of HarperCollins Christian Publishing, Inc.

Requests for information should be addressed to customercare@harpercollins.com.

Zondervan titles may be purchased in bulk for educational, business, fundraising, or sales promotional use. For information, please email SpecialMarkets@Zondervan.com.

ISBN 978-0-310-17724-1 (audio)

Library of Congress Cataloging-in-Publication Data

Names: Palmer, Chris, 1984- author
Title: A world without God : the search for meaning in a society overwhelmed by despair / Chris Palmer.
Description: Grand Rapids, MI : Zondervan Reflective, [2026]
Identifiers: LCCN 2025047087 (print) | LCCN 2025047088 (ebook) | ISBN 9780310177227 paperback | ISBN 9780310177234 ebook
Subjects: LCSH: Life--Religious aspects--Christianity | Meaning (Philosophy)--Religious aspects--Christianity
Classification: LCC BT696 .P35 2026 (print) | LCC BT696 (ebook)
LC record available at https://lccn.loc.gov/2025047087
LC ebook record available at https://lccn.loc.gov/2025047088

HarperCollins Publishers, Macken House, 39/40 Mayor Street Upper, Dublin 1, D01 C9W8, Ireland (https://www.harpercollins.com)

Cover design: Faceout Studio
Cover photo and art: Arnold Böcklin / Public Domain
Interior design: Sara Guild

Printed in the United States of America

26 27 28 29 30 LBC 5 4 3 2 1

To my students

The weariness, the fever, and the fret
Here, where men sit and hear each other groan; . . .
Where but to think is to be full of sorrow
And leaden-eyed despairs,

—John Keats, "Ode to a Nightingale"

CONTENTS

FOREWORD

There is a case to be made that the triumph of Christianity in the Western world opened the door for widespread atheism. Once Christ had vanquished from the field all the old gods from the old world, the new world inaugurated by Christ was only one god away from atheism. After all, it is only a very careful atheist who says, "I don't believe in the gods." No, in the world after Easter it's only one God in which the atheist disbelieves—for only one God has been left standing. Some saw this curious Christian proximity to atheism as an opportunity to be seized, and thus with Nietzsche and his madman announcing the death of God, a bold experiment was embarked upon: a world without God.

The idea was that the last impediment to be overcome by science and technology was the stubborn superstition of belief in God. With the old superstition eradicated, new possibilities would appear. As Ivan Karamazov said, "Without God all things are permitted." Sure, Dostoevsky intended this as a warning, but maybe the axiom could be embraced as aspirational. The experiment in atheism reached its hubristic pinnacle early in the twenty-first century as the four horsemen of the atheist apocalypse galloped their way to fame and onto *The New York Times* bestsellers list. Hitchens, Dawkins, Dennet, and Harris were smug in their self-assurance that the bold experiment was on the verge of complete success.

But Nietzsche himself had never been so confident. Friedrich Nietzche (the colossal thinker of which the new atheists were only cheap imitations) was circumspectly nervous about launching into a world without God. He described it as "unchaining the world from its sun." A risky venture indeed. Nevertheless Nietzsche advocated the uncoupling of humanity from its God. His hope was for mankind to rise to godlike status through the will to power. This is Nietzsche's infamous *Übermensch.* I say infamous, because once Nietzsche's superman goose-stepped onto the world stage asserting will to power over the weak, the *Übermensch* turned out to be not a glorious god but a hideous demon. I realize some philosophers object to associating Nietzsche with Nazis, but it cannot be denied that German fascists from that era took Nietzsche seriously, making books like *Beyond Good and Evil*, *The Antichrist*, and *The Will to Power* canonical texts for national socialism. If, as Jacques Derrida observed, "the only politics calling itself—proclaiming itself—Nietzschean will have been a Nazi one, then this is necessarily significant and must be questioned in all of its consequences."

Nietzsche's *hope* was for the *Übermensch* unshackled from what he called the "slave morality" of Christian love to create a new mankind willing itself to heroic greatness. But Nietzsche's *fear* was that instead of producing the superman, a world without God would only produce the Last Man—Nietzsche's description of a final and failed stage of human development. Nietzsche's Last Man is an incurious, bored, oversedated, entertainment-addled dolt muttering "we have invented happiness" as he stupidly blinks. Might we begin to think that Nietzsche's experiment of a world without God doesn't lead to the godlike superman but to the endlessly scrolling screen-man? As the evidence mounts, we can see the writing on the wall—*mene, mene, tekel, upharsin.* Atheism has been weighed in the balance and found wanting.

Welcome to Novemberton. (Chris Palmer will explain.)

In Palmer's *A World Without God* we find a fascinating convergence of philosophy, sociology, theology, and literary fiction. For example, characters from Dostoevsky's *Crime and Punishment*, *Demons*, and *The Brothers Karamazov* give university lectures while the underground man himself from Dostoevsky's *Notes* is the campus IT. Brilliant and darkly funny! In Palmer's fictional (but all too real) society overwhelmed by despair, the enigmatic line from Dostoevsky's *The Idiot* hangs in the air like a single, clear note from a forgotten church bell: "Beauty will save the world." In his Nobel Lecture, Aleksandr Solzenitsyn said Doestevsky's famous line wasn't a riddle but a prophecy. A century and a half after the openhearted and guileless Prince Myshkin suggested that beauty will save the world, maybe we can glimpse the first hints of the prophecy beginning to come to pass.

But alas, let us not rush too far ahead. Instead let us begin in the dreary streets of Novemberton with Chris Palmer as our capable guide. He has much to show us, and all of it is important.

—Brian Zahnd, author of *When Everything's on Fire*, All Hallows Eve, 2025

PROLOGUE

It wasn't supposed to feel like this.

By all accounts, life was working. The PhD, the perfect job, the house on a lake—everything straight from the script. Earning more, moving forward—crossing off goals. I built a life that looked good on paper. But paper doesn't hold weight when grief hits.

That November, my mother was sick. The kind of sick that makes you feel twelve years old again—helpless, unqualified, waiting for an adult to tell you what to do. I was suddenly aware that every moment is borrowed. I had been sitting with her for hours, watching her. On my way home, I left the room and wandered down the hospital hallway, filled with grief.

Then I saw the sign:

Chapel.

I opened the door.

It was small. Still. Beige walls, worn chairs, a wooden cross fixed to a plain wall. The kind of room I'd ignored before. But in that moment, I needed somewhere quiet to be small.

So I sat.

I didn't stop believing. Not even then. But faith doesn't always feel like a fire. Sometimes it flickers. Sometimes it just rests—tired, steady, aching for breath. That's where I was. I didn't need to be convinced. I just needed to listen.

And I thought about the world, this brilliant, exhausted world. The screens and the arguments, the irony and ambition. The endless scroll. So much noise and so much anguish.

So many people chasing something and not knowing what they're missing.

What if they aren't just tired? What if they've forgotten what it is to be upheld?

That night, Novemberton came to me.

Not as a dream. Not as a sermon. As a town shaped by absence, unsettled and at times absurd. A place where people still reach but don't know what for. Where faith isn't mocked, just forgotten. Misplaced.

This book isn't a map. It's a walk through that town. Through questions. Through weariness. Through a chaos that doesn't care. Godless. Listening, but not hearing.

I wrote this book for those who aren't sure what they believe anymore. And for those, like me, who do believe but are tired, aching, and unsure how to move through a world that grows heavier by the day.

I left the chapel and went home in silence. No music. No noise. Just a quiet weight pressing beneath everything else.

That night, I sat and tried to name the uneasiness. Not to define it but to see it. The ache of a world that still moves but has forgotten where it's going. And as I wrote, a town began to take shape.

This book doesn't fit neatly into a category.

It is not a novel. Not only philosophy. Not simply theology. It is also literary, intuitive, and haunted by questions that each of us may face.

It moves between two worlds: the internal landscape of the town you will visit, shaped by absence, memory, and longing; and the external world we all inhabit, with its headlines, histories, and the slow disintegration of belief.

Novemberton is imagined, but it is not unreal. It is a place built from questions, sorrow, fragments of culture, and the fading outlines of faith. At its core, the darkness isn't the absence of God but the absence of our sight.

Throughout each chapter, you will find many voices: poets, philosophers, theologians, wanderers. And my own. I do not stand above the book. I am walking through it and inviting you into the journey. This is a shared unfolding, one of witness and wonder, equal parts reflection and diagnosis. I hope it moves you. I hope it unsettles you. I hope you breathe out slowly when you finish, place the book on a shelf, and return to it whenever the ghost whispers again.

It is a town I call Novemberton. A world without God.

You may recognize it.

It may be closer than you think.

Chapter One

NOVEMBER OF THE SOUL

Whenever I find myself growing grim about the mouth; whenever it is a damp drizzly November in my soul; whenever I find myself involuntarily pausing before coffin warehouses, and bringing up the rear of every funeral I meet; and especially whenever my hypos gets such an upper hand of me . . . then, I account it high time to get to sea as soon as I can.

—Herman Melville, *Moby-Dick*

Lake Superior is a foreboding riddle.

Don't mistake the angry abyss for its serene shallows. Its depths await to feed on those who underestimate its temper.

I once asked my father what's beneath the surface of the steel-gray chasm.

"Graves," he said.

I looked out at the lurching waves being stirred into a force below the now-dark hue of pitch-black clouds and reserved any further query.

Dad was referring to the *Edmund Fitzgerald*.

Those two words still unnerve the Michigan locals.

Gordon Lightfoot sings about the fateful voyage through folk ballad in "The Wreck of the Edmund Fitzgerald." The song describes a large freighter, well staffed and captained, departing with a steel shipment to Cleveland. Later that night, amid rising winds, something goes wrong. The ship may have broken apart, capsized, or sunk in deep water. No one knows for sure. All that remains are the memories and names of those lost, their families left behind.

The storm that took it wasn't just weather. Locals speak of it like a force, sudden and ravenous. The dawn arrived late that day, and ordinary life was suspended. Meals were forgotten. The November wind tore across the lake like a blade. Some say November itself came alive, not as a date but as a devourer.

No one will ever know what happened when the *Edmund Fitzgerald* dissolved into the stomach of Lake Superior on that fateful night. But one thing is certain:

It happened in November.

A NOVEMBER SORT OF VIBE

If you've read *Moby-Dick*, you might recall the story begins with the narrator, Ishmael, reflecting on the month of November. The coming of winter has brought him sadness. He reflects on death. Melancholy gets the best of him. Ishmael considers joining a whaling voyage to keep from staring at coffins.

The author of *Moby-Dick*, Herman Melville, uses November as a stark symbol to point at something more than the weather. "November of the soul" refers to the anxiety that the characters in the story suffer. It is the drooping mood of anguish; the sinking feeling of futility; the tumbling stir of insignificance. It's the numbness of pointlessness. Meaninglessness. It's the sort of state that causes you to visit cemeteries in your free time.

November swallows the soul like it's the *Edmund Fitzgerald*.

The writer of Ecclesiastes suffered from the November of the soul. His book about life, oddly, starts with his grim conclusion: "Meaningless! Meaningless! . . . Utterly meaningless!" (Eccl. 1:2).

Quite a statement to begin with. "Utterly meaningless" also reads "meaninglessness of meaninglessness." The Hebrew is emphatic: "vanity of vanities," the emptiest of the empty. It's as if the writer is saying there is nothing more meaningless than this.

Both the writer of Ecclesiastes and Ishmael connect the mood of anguish with the meaninglessness of life.

The writer of Ecclesiastes admits that searching for meaning leads only to more grief: "For with much wisdom comes much sorrow; the more knowledge, the more grief" (v. 18).

This mirrors Ishmael's perspective as he observes Captain Ahab's obsessive pursuit of the white whale and reflects on how humans, in their attempts to comprehend what lies beyond them, ultimately spiral into madness.

Ahab's quest for the white whale is a metaphor for humankind's search for meaning, a search that ends with a troubled soul.

A troubled soul changes the way you see life. Optimism is a facade and pessimism a smokescreen. Both are distractions and defense mechanisms to keep you from having to deal with the pointlessness of life that Ishmael and the writer of Ecclesiastes wrestle with. An optimist will tell you the glass is half full and a pessimist will tell you it's half empty. But the Novemberist with the troubled soul will suggest you throw the glass away, because who even cares? After all, it doesn't really matter. As horrible as it sounds, when you search for meaning, that's how the search ends.

Alan Watts, a philosopher and entertainer, summed up his search for meaning by saying "it has become extremely plausible that this trip between the maternity ward and the crematorium *is* what there is to life."[1] Sounds like an old humorous saying David Gerrold, the screenwriter, reminded us of: "Life is hard.

Then you die. They throw dirt in your face. Then the worms eat you. Be grateful it happens in that order."[2]

One notorious Novemberist who embraced, rather radically, the pointlessness of life is Emil Cioran. Cioran lived his life as a failure, on purpose. He had no practical ambitions, wandered around Paris aimlessly without ever having a real job, and crudely said that the only ones more idle than him were "prostitutes without clients." The November of his soul was so vexing that he found no worth in trying only for it to end in death. In his book *The Trouble with Being Born*, he says, "I used to ask myself, over a coffin: 'what good did it do the occupant to be born?' I now ask the same question about anyone alive."[3]

In act 5, scene 5 of Shakespeare's *Macbeth*, Macbeth learns of the death of his wife and faces the November of his own soul. His reflection sums up Cioran, Gerrold, Watts, Ishmael, and the writer of Ecclesiastes. It expresses the attitude of the Novemberist who has gone about Novemberton in search of a point to it all:

> Life's but a walking shadow, a poor player
> That struts and frets his hour upon the stage
> And then is heard no more. It is a tale
> Told by an idiot, full of fury,
> Signifying nothing.[4]

A TOWN COME OF AGE

To understand Novemberton, you have to acquaint yourself with the important observation that Dietrich Bonhoeffer made about the world he knew. Bonhoeffer lived in the early twentieth century. During his thirty-nine years of life (1906–45), a lot of scientific and engineering advances were taking place. Big ones. The electron had just been discovered. Einstein developed his theory of relativity. The Wright brothers and Lindbergh took flight. The Empire State Building went up. The Hoover Dam was completed. People were getting into Model Ts. Scientific progress and civil engineering led to the development of the A-bomb that fell over Japan just 119 days after Bonhoeffer's death.

Bonhoeffer described his world as a world that had "come of age." To come of age means to grow up and mature. As a result, you no longer need the things you needed while you were young. Think of a child who takes off her training wheels. Bonhoeffer believed the world had grown, and that it would soon put its training wheels on the shelf. These training wheels were the perceptions people had about God prior to the explosion of human achievement. "God is being increasingly pushed out of a world that has come of age, out of the spheres of our knowledge and life."[5]

Bonhoeffer was suggesting that people were no longer naïve. Simple, religious answers about God would no longer be suitable to account for the world's growing complexity. These had been put up for a more "grown up" approach to life.

Imagine trying to explain to an adult that the sun goes to bed at night when it gets dark. It works with your four-year-old to get them to fall asleep. But as soon as they have first-grade science, the jig is up. You'll have to figure out a new way to get them to zonk out.

In Novemberton, everyone has come of age. Simple, ordinary explanations are incompatible with the world they inhabit, which now includes enough warheads to blow the earth off of its orbit, and cars that drive themselves. What's all this progress mean? They aren't sure. But "God" feels like a bedtime story. The story is nice to think about, but it's incompatible with the world.

This grown-up world might have some meaning, but it does not have *the* meaning. Something has been lost, not mourned, discarded. Faith has been laid aside like training wheels, and meaning, once grounded in God, now floats untethered. The town doesn't wait. It moves, distracted and hollow, unaware that anything is missing at all.

THE TOWN WAITS

I find myself on Novemberton's streets before I fully realize I've arrived. It's like walking into a room that has been waiting for you.

Along the street, figures bustle in and out of view like unraveling threads. A woman stands on the curb, a sign trembling in her hands: "Save Mother Earth!" Across from her, a boy kneels on the pavement, shuffling tarot cards slowly and deliberately, turning them over, frowning and reshuffling. I glance away, drawn toward a café glowing dimly in the rain. The thought of hot coffee warms me.

Inside, the air is sweet with something herbal, spiced, cinnamon perhaps. A woman at the next table exhales a long, burdened sigh, her fingers moving ceaselessly over the glass of her phone. There's something about her, weary, sad, lost even. Her gaze catches mine a moment too long, and for a second, I think we might speak. But her expression falters and she turns back to the glow, dim and narcotic, like a nightlight for the restless.

I peer round. Near the counter, a student turns a folded flyer in his hands, the black letters just visible: "The Principles for a Human Religion: A Panel Discussion." Above him, a dream catcher trembles in the draft. Every face in the room carries a kind of quiet restlessness, like they're all waiting for something that never arrives. Each choice seems haunted by the one that follows.

The door swings open and cold air needles the skin on my neck. A man steps inside. No hesitation. His suit is cheap but pressed, his shoes dull but clean. He orders black coffee, drinks it without letting it cool. When he finishes, he sets the cup down with a kind of finality, then simply sits there, watching. He unsettles me. It's not the way he looks at the room, it's the absence of something behind his eyes. Not because he's searching. Because he isn't.

I leave before finishing my drink.

The street has folded back around itself, damp and close. Winter has settled here—not just in the air, not just in the bones of the town, but deeper still. I see it in people's faces, in the way people move, in the way they hesitate.

I step off the curb without looking. A driver sputters by; his horn jolts my chest and I stumble back, heart hammering. The car swerves past, the driver's face blank behind the glass.

Shaken, I glance down, fumbling for something solid. My phone lights up in my hand.

November 1st.

I take a breath and step back, not from the street but from the moment. What am I seeing here? What is this place?

In Novemberton, four things have become painfully clear.

1. There Is Still a Search for a Higher Meaning

Novemberton isn't an island. The town is linked to the rest of the world, tangled in a globalized web of markets and media. Everyone drinks Colombian coffee and wears T-shirts made in Vietnam. They walk past their neighbors yet send heart emojis across oceans. My brief time at the café and walking through town has opened my eyes to the townspeople's wide interests and endless search for something new. They know international politics and watch Japanese anime with subtitles. They hope to try authentic pho one day. Something real.

And yet the search doesn't stop there. It never stops. This is a town of seekers.

There's a strange form of spirituality here, one without God, yet the city is thick with gods—small, fleeting, shifting with the wind. Each new interest is a temporary light, a momentary warmth until it fades and they move on. They cannot settle because there is always another path, another possibility, another answer.

2. The Townspeople Are Apathetic and Bored

For all their longing for higher meaning, apathy is pervasive among this culture. Bo Burnham's rise to popularity with songs like "All Eyes on Me" captures this indifference perfectly. He sings about rising oceans, collapsing futures, and panic attacks, describing a world unraveling, yet a self too exhausted and numb to respond.

Bo wrote this song while battling a crisis of meaning that intensified during the pandemic. Like all art, Bo's Grammy-winning song is open to interpretation. The song's panic resonates with those who feel the world is broken and the future is beyond repair. One of his fans says, "To me this song represents the struggle to continue to care when caring is exhausting."[6]

The youth, in particular, no longer care. They gave up plastic straws while celebrities flew in private jets. They worked hard in university, racking up bills that will take fifteen years to pay.[7] Their parents said to work hard. Save. Stop buying fraps! But frap or no frap, they are priced out of traditional markers of success, like buying a house and a car.[8]

Now they reach for cigarettes instead of the future.[9] Nicotine pouches are in.[10] Laissez-faire vibes grow in spite of draconian wellness campaigns. The merit system is a sham. Cross every *t*, dot every *i*, but you'll still fall short. So screw your dreams. You can't have a car, but you can buy a nicotine high to make the bus ride bearable. Prioritize comfort: Exchange goals and values for immediate relief. Apathy is the play. Care less.

Luxury markets have gotten smaller; youth prefer fashion they can afford.[11] Thrifting and customizable experiences, like blind boxes, are in. Hustle culture is cringe. The twenty-two-year-old start-up guru who claims to have made millions in "just a few months!" is loathed. The #girlboss has been fired and replaced by #lazygirljobs.

Humor has grown darker. Tragedies that once felt untouchable, like 9/11, have become fodder for comedy, stripped of reverence, turned to punch lines.

The prospect of self-annihilation is now casually floated as a climate solution. "Mother Earth might throw a party," someone quips online, suggesting human extinction as eco-salvation.

Apparently wiping ourselves off the map is the best way to return the earth to harmony.

Most shocking is the unabashed scorn people openly direct toward little children. It's as if the innocence and vulnerability of children is reduced to something unworthy of life. It's a disturbing reflection of how detached Novemberton has become from caring.

The entertainment industry is also affected by the indifference. The names of entertainers and influencers resemble cryptic AIM usernames: A$AP Rocky, Doja Cat, PewDiePie, MrBeast. These monikers act as digital masks. They ignite viral intrigue, revealing just enough to capture attention while keeping identity a mystery.

Hookup culture has become second nature—sex stripped of emotional attachment, somatic connection unbothered by the burden of intimacy. Sex is nothing more than a transaction, devoid of deeper meaning. Porn has played a significant role in cheapening sex.[12] Adult creators push the boundaries of sexual detachment through provocative stunts like attempting to break the world record for the most people they can sleep with in a single day.[13]

3. There Is a Growing Lack of Commitment to Things

Sh. Don't say the *c* word too loud. Commitment makes the townspeople nervous. Commitments are risky. Something is on the line. There are endless ways to opt out of commitment. Get your tubes tied.[14] Ditch marriage for polyamory.[15] Ghost that person you've been texting for three months.[16] Breakup talks are hard and require vulnerability. In the words of Sweet Brown, "Ain't nobody got time for that!"

Many are awakening to the reality of the hamster wheel. Going into the office to drink the same stale coffee, Monday after Monday, is a commitment too steep to keep. The wheel will keep spinning as long as one lets it. That's why more folks are getting off.[17] And those who aren't are all but giving up on their commitment to their workplace's vision statement. Bad service is everywhere you go: the café, the restaurant. God forbid you'll need your internet fixed. If a worker has no other choice but to exchange their life force for a corporate strategy, they sure as heck aren't going to do it with efficiency or a smile on their face. Not for trash pay. Businesses promise you the world, but good luck getting a hot burger. The high expectations of customers, created by corporations, are deflated by the unreliability of customer service in the industry.[18]

It's interesting. They've never known more. But there's a hesitancy to do anything with that information. If there's any commitment, it's to idle curiosity.

4. Meeting Base Needs Is the Townspeople's Priority

In my own life, I saw this lack of commitment up close. In 2024, Hurricane Milton blew through central Florida. I had just moved there. It was just my luck that within the first three months of Florida livin', Tampa faced its first direct hit from a hurricane since 1921. Even the locals fled. If you aren't familiar with Florida culture, that's rare. The Waffle Houses shut down, for heaven's sake! But the popular IG meme page @floridaman identified one unlikely hero: DoorDash. Out there in the 120 mph winds there was a lone doordasher dropping off sliders. (Okay, maybe not all customer service is bad.) Someone left a comment saying, "I don't care if Tampa gets destroyed. I want my grub!"

This comment reminded me of the dark humor of "the Underground Man" in Fyodor Dostoyevsky's *Notes from Underground*. The Underground Man's town is rotten and, all too often, feels meaningless. He says, "The whole world can go to hell, but I shall have my tea." Literary critics have spent a lot of time reflecting on what the vile misanthrope meant. I think he means the same thing the Florida commenter did:

The world is a horrible place where things are falling apart. The only right move is to cling to your comforts. Withdraw into your solitary pleasures. You can't change the world. You're entitled to whatever relief you can get. Focus on your sliders. Tea is your only escape.

THE BELLS ECHO SILENTLY

As I wander, I find myself outside a church slouching in abandonment.[19] There are no bells, just silence, and a forlorn facade, welcoming no one.

I climb the steps and press the door. To my surprise, it isn't locked. A faded notice clings to a bulletin board: "Easter Service." Below it, an old wedding photo, sun-bleached and brittle, showing pastel dresses, confetti in the air, a priest smiling beneath the weight of years. All from a time gone by.

There's something beneath all this strangeness. A current, a question, and I want to find it. Not just to see but to understand. Novemberton may feel like a busy, restless town, but I suspect it's something more. A mirror, maybe. Or a warning. I don't know. But either way, I must look.

This isn't just a visit. It's a search.

I step inside; the air is cool and thick dust lingers on each surface. I walk slowly down the aisle, my footsteps muffled by a hush that clings to places like this. A woman sits alone, staring up at the stained-glass window. Its fractured reds and blues rest dully across the empty pews, and I wonder if she remembers that time. "I just come here to think," she whispers, hearing my steps.

The people of Novemberton wear their burdens openly—heavy lines etched into their faces, hollows dark beneath their eyes. It's not just tiredness. I wonder if they notice it anymore. They move through their days like sleepwalkers, tethered to routine, to duty, and to some vague idea of more they can never quite define. Despite all the advances in science and technology, they remain bored, unsatisfied, and unable to muster much of a commitment to anything. DoorDash is their lifeline, their buoy in the rising waters of November. And they know, though they never say it, that the water is rising.

But there she is. Just one more weary soul in Novemberton, sitting in a chapel, not for answers but for some quiet.

I step back into the gray, past the faded photo, the forgotten notice, leaving her there with the echo of bells long rung out. Outside, the wind stirs, restless, tugging at the brittle leaves and the corners of the old flyers.

Novemberton breathes, I think.

There are still other places to look, other doors to press. But something in the way she sat there, still, listening, told me I'm not the only one searching.

SITTING IN A CHAPEL

Jack Higgins was a British author who achieved peak success with his popular espionage thrillers. His novel *The Eagle Has Landed* sold more than fifty million copies and later became a movie. Do you realize how many copies fifty million is? Less than 2 percent of books sell more than fifty thousand copies. Those of us who only dream to achieve this sort of prestige and fame—nowadays as influencers—take for granted that a sense of higher meaning and purpose simply comes along with it. Jack warns that it doesn't. "I wish someone had told me that when you get to the top, there's nothing there."

There's a certain irony about achievement, the kind that ushers in a November of the soul. Whether it's a personal triumph or the collective achievement of society, it always ends with a quiet, dull emptiness that lingers long after the celebration fades.

Have you experienced this? I think we all have. The writer of Ecclesiastes certainly did. In chapter 2 of his book, he lists all of his accomplishments. We're talking big sprawling homes with intricate, designer interiors. Cutting-edge technology. Commanding networks of booming businesses. The glitter of fame. Agency. There was no one who wouldn't take his calls.[20] He was like the entrepreneurial mogul who shows up on your explore page and offers a one-minute business strategy that promises to change everything.

Like Jack Higgins, he says, "Yet when I surveyed all that my hands had done and what I had toiled to achieve, everything was meaningless, a chasing after the wind; nothing was gained under the sun" (Eccl. 2:11). Perhaps the writer of Ecclesiastes had that grim state in his eyes while he assessed his achievements.

DOVER BEACH

In 1867, Matthew Arnold published a poem titled "Dover Beach." Like Bonhoeffer, Arnold noticed that human achievement had troubled faith.

The poem reminds me of a day at Lake Superior. The poet admires the splendid landscape that surrounds the sea. He can see the coasts of England and France. How magnificent and splendid!

> The sea is calm tonight.
> The tide is full, the mood lies fair
> Upon the straights; on the French coast the light
> Gleams and is gone; the cliffs of England stand,
> Glimmering and vast, out in the tranquil bay.

And yet the longer he observes the coast and the sea, the more unease takes hold.

> The Sea of Faith
> Was once, too, at the full, and round earth's shore
> Lay like the folds of a bright girdle furled.

But now I only hear
Its melancholy, long, withdrawing roar,
Retreating, to the breath
Of the night-wind, down the vast edges drear
And naked shingles of the world.

The sea illustrates the world's loss of faith. Like the tide, belief in God has slowly receded, driven away by the wake of progress and human achievement. There was a time when God gave humanity purpose and a sense of comfort. But faith was eroding, the world was being left naked, vulnerable to the despair that comes from wondering whether there's even a point to life.

The last lines of the poem give the reader insight into what the poet thinks a world without God—and the meaning that comes from faith in God—is destined to become.

And we are here as on a darkling plain
Swept with confused alarms of struggle and flight,
Where ignorant armies clash by night.[21]

The "darkling plain" is a horrifying place. It is Novemberton. While it is full of advances, it is full of "alarms" and "struggle." There is widespread panic. Arnold predicts modernization will bring with it a significant increase in violence. Doubtless, the world's supply of nuclear warheads would not surprise him.

To summarize, the poet makes three observations about the modern age that the average person in the twenty-first century has come to face:

1. God feels untenable.
2. The search for meaning seems impossible.
3. Living is fierce.

If you're honest with yourself, have you had any one of these three thoughts in the last year? Month? Week? How ironic considering how much humankind has made strides to improve itself.

Without God, society is certain to sink like the *Edmund Fitzgerald*. We may find a cure for cancer. It's likely we'll soon get to Mars. Your great-grandkids will probably never have to steer a car, and driver related fatalities will diminish. But will the latest technologies offer us a reason for it all? The forecast is unlikely.

In the chapters ahead, we will journey the darkling plains, this world without God. How did it become this way? How does the human psyche bear such a burden? Where shall we find our values? Morality? Is there a way forward, or should we all give up and let ourselves free-fall to the bottom of the sea?

To answer these questions, we must begin with Novemberton and how it came to be. It didn't happen overnight. As Arnold has pointed out, it was through a slow erosion. Once, humankind assumed the presence of a creator. But over time, God found himself in the acid bath, disintegrating in the corrosive decay of human thought.

— Chapter Two —

GOD IN THE ACID BATH

God is dead. God remains dead. And we have killed him. How shall we comfort ourselves, the murderers of all murderers?

—The madman, *Thus Spoke Zarathustra*

The buildings here lean inward, like they've grown tired of holding themselves up.

I find myself in front of the library. It doesn't look abandoned, not entirely, but it remembers how to be quiet. It rises from the street, vines clawing at its stone, and wears a cracked sign that still carries its name.

Inside, the air tells of memories and forgotten things and holds a faint lingering scent of paper left untouched for too long. Rows of books stand like sentries, keeping watch over ideas no one seems to need anymore.

I came here looking for answers. I wasn't sure about what kind, but some explanation for why the soul feels heavier now than it used to.

I walk slowly between the shelves. The words of the old thinkers still live here, but barely. I pull a volume from the shelf, more worn than the others, and flip it open. Its spine cracks. It feels like a confession.

Its name, *The Joyous Science*, and the author is Friedrich Nietzsche. Nietzsche is a German philosopher who lived in the nineteenth century.

Even if you've never read him, you've heard the quote: "God is dead." It's a cliché now, thrown around too easily. But here, in this town, in this moment, it feels like a funeral rite.

The passage comes from a section titled "The Madman." A parable. A prophet, deranged and glowing, enters a town square—a place not unlike Novemberton—and begins to cry out.

> Have you not heard of that madman who lit a lantern in the bright morning light, ran to the marketplace and shouted incessantly, "I seek God! I seek God!" As there were many people standing together who did not believe in God, he caused much amusement. "Is he lost?" asked one. "Did he wander off like a child?" asked another. "Or is he hiding? Is he afraid of us? Has he gone to sea? Has he emigrated?" And in this manner they shouted and laughed. . . .
>
> Then the madman leaped into their midst, and looked at them with piercing eyes and cried, "Where did God go? I will tell you! We have killed him—you and I! We are all his murderers. But how did we do this? . . .
>
> "Are we not constantly falling? Backward, sideward, forward, in all directions? Is there still an above and below? . . . Do we hear nothing yet of the noise of the gravediggers who are burying God? Do we smell nothing yet of the divine putrefaction? For even gods putrefy! God is dead. God remains dead. And we have killed him!"

The panic in his voice grows. The madness is not from delusion but from knowing exactly what's been lost:

> "How shall we, the most murderous of all murderers, ever console ourselves? The holiest and mightiest thing that the world

> has ever known has bled to death under our knives—who will wash this blood clean from our hands . . . What lustrations, what sacred games shall we have to invent . . . Must we not become gods ourselves, if only to appear worthy of it?"
>
> It is said that on that very day, the madman made his way into various churches, and there intoned his *requiem aeternam deo* [prayer for the deceased]. When led out and called to account, he always replied, "What are these churches now, if not the tombs and sepulchres of God?"[1]

I close the book. My hands feel cold. The silence in the library deepens—not peaceful but charged.

Now I understand.

With every page, a quiet panic creeps up my spine.

Not because the madman is wrong.

But because I think he's right:

1. *Humans killed God.* "We have killed him . . . We are all his murderers." Society is responsible. God's blood is upon humanity's sword.
2. *Humans have lost meaning.* "Are we not constantly falling?" Society realizes that God is what gave them their sense of meaning. With God now dead, society is left without a guiding force to provide it with a sense of lasting significance. The former values can no longer do. Society is left with that sinking feeling—the November of the soul—and it plunges into despair.
3. *Humans have taken God's place.* "What lustrations, what sacred games shall we have to invent? . . . Must we not become gods ourselves, if only to appear worthy of it?" After the gravedigger has thrown his final heap of earth onto God's coffin, society faces a choice: (a) succumb to the despair of having no ultimate significance beyond God or (b) rise from the November of its soul and create its own values to shape its own meaning in a world that was once defined by the divine.

In other words, be overcome by the death of God or become your own god.

THE STORY OF THE JUDGES

The revelation lands heavily, pressing into me.

I lay the book down.

I look for a Bible and find one. Another cracked spine, cover faded and corners curled from years of disuse. Still, it opens easily, like it remembers the shape of hands.

It occurs to me that there was, at least once in human history, a time when society tried to become its own God.

I start turning pages, breathing in the musty scent of old paper and ink. Yellowed pages beneath my thumbs as my eyes scan in quick, searching rhythm. Then I stop.

Judges.

The words pull at me.

I sit down. The bench is hard and cold, but I don't notice right away. The story rises from the page like heat from the ground. My heart picks up pace. There's something here, something that mirrors the madman's cry in Nietzsche's square. A people without center. A culture unraveling. Not by violence but by forgetting.

Again, three things strike me:

1. The people have killed God.
    - "Then the Israelites did evil in the eyes of the Lord and served the Baals. They forsook [abandoned] the Lord" (Judg. 2:11–12).
    - Abandonment. The people of Israel have kicked dirt onto God's grave. They have moved forward with unwavering steps and left his memory to fade.
2. The people search for new meaning.
    - "They quickly turned from the ways of their ancestors, who had been obedient to the Lord's commands" (2:17).

  - After the death of God, former values are forsaken. A new way of life emerges.
3. The people take God's place.
  - "Everyone did as they saw fit" (21:25).
  - A chill works its way down my spine. I know this line. I've quoted it. But now, in the silence of the library, it doesn't feel like a summary. It feels like a diagnosis.

Judges turns out to be a dark story. It is filled with violence and bloodshed, rape, betrayal, and moral decay. There is even a story wherein a man, named Jephthah, sacrifices his own daughter (11:29–40).

How could someone do such a thing? What is right is determined by the values the people have invented themselves. This is the new way of life that has emerged. The twisted stories in Judges illustrate the chaos that follows this new way of life, when humanity takes God's place. Seeking to author new meaning, the people of Israel find only more despair in the world without God they have created.

A WORLD WITHOUT GOD IS A MOOD

Mood is not just an inner feeling, it is the atmosphere through which the world reveals itself. It shapes what we notice, how we interpret events, and what we believe is true or possible. In this way, mood becomes a kind of lived epistemology—a way of knowing shaped by our experience—not only coloring what we feel but structuring how we understand the world.

In the same way, entire societies live within moods—atmospheric ways of making sense of things. These moods shape how people see the world, what they value, what they pursue. And they can change. The parable of the madman captures such a shift: the moment when the death of God signals not just the loss of belief but the arrival of a new mood, one that rearranges meaning. What follows is not just a new set of ideas but a new world, felt and lived differently.

MOOD SWINGS

I rise, unsteady. My footsteps sound too loud in the empty library.

I pace between the shelves, pulling book after book, riffling through pages with desperate urgency. Author after author, meaning has unraveled until nothing remains but the awareness of its absence. I trace the slow disintegration of belief, the erosion of meaning stretched across centuries. From Plato's perfect forms to Descartes's relentless doubt, from the Enlightenment's cold dissection of truth to Nietzsche's final pronouncement: "God is dead. We have killed him." It presses upon me now, an invisible weight. It all makes sense.

At first, I just sit there, staring at the words, rereading them as if repetition might soften their blow. But the meaning is clear. The abandoned churches, the lost expressions, the gnawing, ceaseless ache of the town suddenly make sense in a way that makes me shudder.

If God was slowly dipped in the acid bath, layer by layer, then God has disintegrated.

I try to grasp it all. How did it come to this?

1. The Mood of the Gods[2]

In the beginning, there was God.

At first, human history supposes that there is a divine, transcendent being (or beings) responsible for the creation of the world and all things therein. While holy books differ as to who or what "god" is, the single unifier is that god *is*. Humans come from God; humans end with God. The most influential books from early human history assume this: the Hebrew Bible, the *Epic of Gilgamesh*, and Homer's writings. And while these holy books aren't unified on the nature of God, God is always superhuman—above humans in power and authority.

During the mood of the gods, superhuman beings shaped the moral and life-related instructions by which humans lived. When one's life is aligned with divine instruction, it creates a sense of purpose and significance.

In the Hebrew Bible, the book which ponders meaning and purpose, Ecclesiastes, sums up its exploration with a call to obey God's instructions. "Now all has been heard; here is the conclusion of the matter: Fear God and keep his commandments, for this is the duty of all mankind" (Eccl. 12:13).

The writer of Ecclesiastes goes so far as to say that obedience to God is everyone's ultimate duty. I uncover that *duty* is a Hebrew idiom, and it literally means "this is the whole of humanity." "Obeying God is the most important thing that anyone can do"[3] if they would like a meaningful life.

In the *Epic of Gilgamesh*, I see a similar emphasis on obedience to divine instruction. In one story, a great flood is coming to destroy mankind. Ea, one of the principal Mesopotamian gods, warns a man named Utnapishtim and instructs him to tear down his house of reeds and to use those reeds to make a boat. Utnapishtim obeys without hesitancy. He tells Ea, "Behold, what you have commanded I will honor and perform."[4]

The flood comes and devastates the world for six days and six nights. Utnapishtim and his wife are the only humans who survive. When the flood subsides, Enlil, another Mesopotamian god, grants Utnapishtim and his wife immortality for their obedience to the gods. In the *Epic of Gilgamesh*, obeying divine guidance is connected to human flourishing.

I learn that the writings of Homer are no different as they teach the importance of being in harmony with divine instruction. In *The Odyssey*, you come across the story of Odysseus and the Sirens. In this story, a sorceress/goddess named Circe informs Odysseus about the dangers he and his men will face on their way home from the underworld. The songs of the Sirens will lead to ruin. She implores Odysseus, "Your descent to the dead is over, true, but listen closely to what I tell you now and god himself will bring it back to mind. First you will raise the island of the Sirens, those creatures who spellbind any man alive . . . The high, thrilling song of the Sirens will transfix him, lolling there in their meadow, round them heaps of corpses rotting away, rags of skin shriveling on their bones."[5]

Oof.

Circe instructs the men to plug their ears with beeswax so they don't hear them. If Odysseus wants to listen, he at least needs to be tied to the ship's mast so he doesn't go after the Sirens when they sing their enchanting songs. Her instructions save Odysseus and his men. This story shows how human purpose is associated with divinity during the time of Homer.

What's clear from my survey of these ancient books is that, during the mood of the gods, society valued living in harmony with God or the gods. Divine wisdom and instruction provided humanity the basis for a life of purpose and meaning.

But things don't stay this way. I find that roughly four hundred years after Homer, humanity's understanding of the divine shifts. Suppositions about God become unfastened, creating space for new ideas. An ideological shift occurs, and humankind goes through its first-ever mood swing.

2. The Mood of Reason

I'd heard a lot about Plato before this. But something shifts as I study in the eerie stillness of Novemberton's library. I take him more seriously now. In this dim hush, he becomes more than a name; he becomes part of the slow unraveling that leads to God's death in the acid bath. Plato saw truth as something eternal and objective. Truth wasn't revealed through divine revelation but was something you reasoned toward.

Up until Plato, the gods gave humankind its meaning and value.

But Plato shifts the foundation.

Instead of seeing the gods as the source, Plato argues that truth, justice, and value exist independently in a higher, eternal realm of perfect Forms. He doesn't exactly ditch the divine, just makes it something more abstract—less like Zeus throwing thunderbolts and more like an eternal rational principle governing the universe. This shift is illustrated by his parable of the campfire in *The Republic.*

The fire pulls up memories of childhood bonfires. Under the stars, holding a marshmallow on a stick, my cousin, always a bit of a showoff, says, "Hey, look what I can do!" Placing his hands between his chest and the fire, he casts a shadow that imitates a giant butterfly. For the next hour, all the cousins sit around the fire, making up their own hand-shadow puppets. Those were the days.

This is what goes on in Plato's allegory of the cave. In this tale, prisoners have been chained in a cave their entire lives, forced to face only the wall. Behind them, there is a fire. Men pass between the prisoners and the fire, carrying objects that cast their shadows on the wall. Because the prisoners have only ever seen the wall, they think the shadows are reality. Once a prisoner is freed, he discovers the world outside the cave and realizes the shadows he thought were reality are mere reflections. After a period of adjustment, he grows accustomed to the reality of the world outside and pities those still back in the cave who think the shadows are real.

Imagine you are at a campfire today, and a person believes that a butterfly hand-shadow is actually a butterfly. Wouldn't that seem absurd? You'd want to get that individual some help.

Plato looked at the people around him that way. Take justice, for instance. Is what we call justice today actually justice? I think we can all settle on the fact that justice remains imperfect. Thus, the justice we observe today is just a butterfly shadow. Calling it justice is just as absurd as saying a shadow is the butterfly.

But Plato believed the perfect form of justice did exist. And it existed as a *form*—an essence or nature, an unchanging and timeless ideal. A perfect form cannot be grasped through the five senses. It can be understood only through reason: intellectual pursuit, philosophical inquiry, rational thought, and Socratic questioning.

Beauty. Love. Honor. Good. Everything has a perfect form. The allegory of the cave represents the journey from ignorance to a true understanding of these forms through education and philosophy. This is admitted in the allegory: "The prison-house [cave] is the world of sight, the light of the fire is the sun, and you will not misapprehend me if you interpret the journey upwards to be the ascent of the soul into the intellectual world."[6]

After reading Plato, I realize that he believes salvation comes not from divine intervention but from wisdom. Wisdom enables one to understand the perfect forms, which are true reality. His emphasis is on using reason to grasp higher truths, not just collecting facts or scientific knowledge. This doesn't kill God—not yet. Later Christian thinkers will absorb Plato's Form of the Good into their theology, interpreting it as God himself. But something has changed: Meaning is now something to be discovered through reason rather than revealed directly by the gods. Even if the divine remains, it is now approached through philosophy rather than myth.

Things stay this way for a long time, oscillating between theism and Platonism until the seventeenth century, when René Descartes comes along. Another shift is set in motion; humanity's next great mood swing begins, one that plunges God deeper into the acid bath.

3. The Mood of Certainty

There's a saying I used to toss around as a joke. I remember once, out at dinner with friends, looking at the dessert menu way too intensely. Someone asked, "Well? Are you getting dessert or not?" Without missing a beat, I said, "I think, therefore I am," and laughed too hard at my wit. Sadly, the maître d' didn't even crack a smile.

That joke, of course, quotes René Descartes. Though when Descartes said it, it wasn't meant to be funny. As a Catholic, Descartes saw God as essential to grounding knowledge, but his ideas, unintentionally, set in motion a shift that ended up moving God closer to his death.

René Descartes lived during the Scientific Revolution—a time when people were beginning to question the very ideas I just encountered in Plato. Natural science was becoming the dominant framework for understanding the world. I think of Copernicus, who discovered that the sun—not the earth—was at the center of the universe during this time. That single shift changed everything. Add to that the upheaval of the Protestant Reformation and it's easy to see how skepticism became the defining mood of the age.

Descartes takes the mood of his time and applies the scientific method to philosophy and the question of what is really real. He wanted certainty. And not just certainty, he wanted a way to know how anything could be certain.

I find his work *Meditations of First Philosophy* to be quite heavy. His frustration is evident in his search for something certain in which to ground knowledge, reality, and meaning. "It feels I have fallen unexpectedly into a deep whirlpool which tumbles me around so that I can neither stand on the bottom nor swim to the top . . . Anything which admits of the slightest doubt I will set aside just as if I had found it to be wholly false; and I will proceed in this way until I recognize something certain, or, if nothing else, until I at least recognize for certain that there is no certainty."[7]

Descartes discovered that the only thing whose existence is self-given and self-certain is the "I"—the fact of his own existence. "At last I have discovered it—thought; this alone is inseparable from me. I am, I exist—that is certain. But for how long? As long as I am thinking."[8]

His own existence, proved by the fact that he thinks, is immune to doubt. It meets the demand of his skeptical framework.

But this creates a different problem. If the self's existence is the only thing that is certain and self-given, that means that Yahweh, the pantheon of the gods, or a perfect world of ideal forms is not.

I read on, and as I do, I honestly start to like the guy. I can tell he is a deeply religious man. In his third meditation, he gets to the existence of God. He seems anxious about it. He then turns to force of argument[9] to prove it.

But there's another problem.

In the previous moods, God didn't need an argument. In the beginning, God just was. For Platonists, perfect forms just were. With the rise of skepticism, the existence of God could be sensibly questioned.

Though he meant well, Descartes caused a rearrangement of priorities. The human mind became the judge of all things; even God had to justify his existence to human reason. It never used to be this way.

I notice something strange as the Scientific Revolution gives way to the Enlightenment—an intellectual movement that prioritizes reason, skepticism, and individualism. As the world moves forward with these new standards of thinking, God's existence is no longer a given. Confidence in God quietly erodes. The only thing certain is what the human mind can achieve on its own.

Humankind's salvation now relies on certainty. Without certainty, there can be no meaning. And without the certainty of God's existence, society starts to seriously doubt that it can find meaning in God.

Reading Descartes helps me understand where Novemberton's skepticism toward God comes from. But as I move through the Enlightenment and the thinkers who follow Descartes, I can't find the same despair that clings to Novemberton. The mood of the Enlightenment feels strangely upbeat: Reason will light the way, and science will unlock everything humanity needs.

But beneath all the optimism and lofty promises, it seems they never quite found the certainty Descartes was looking for.

Then I return to the works of Friedrich Nietzsche, and the final pieces fall into place.

There's a familiar sinking feeling in his words, like slipping beneath dark water. His writing drags something to the surface:

a recognition. My thoughts flicker back to the gazes around town—the hollow stares, the compulsive scrolling, the aimless hunger in people's eyes. That quiet, unspoken doubt that clings to the air in Novemberton like smoke.

This is where the last mood swing occurs—the mood around Novemberton. Nietzsche explains it all.

4. The Mood of Meaninglessness

Something I notice is that Nietzsche has a fundamental disagreement with Descartes. So what? Just a little disagreement, right? Wrong. What Nietzsche proposes is enough to close the casket on God.

Descartes had proposed the self as a stable, rational entity for discovering certainty. Nietzsche couldn't disagree more. He says, "A thought comes when 'it' wishes, and not when 'I' wish; so that it is a perversion of the facts of the case to say that the subject 'I' is the condition of the predicate 'think.' One thinks; but that this 'one' is precisely the famous old 'ego,' is, to put it mildly, only a supposition, an assertion, and assuredly not an 'immediate certainty.' After all, one has even gone too far with this 'one thinks'—even the 'one' contains an interpretation of the process, and does not belong to the process itself."[10]

Humans are not merely passive observers of reality. Nietzsche argues that we are interpreters, and our knowledge always reflects a personal spin. The world we think we understand is merely a reflection of individual interpretation. One group might see it as a fight for justice. Another group sees it as a disruption of order. It's the same event, yet people couldn't be more divided. This division challenges the idea of entirely objective human rationality. Nietzsche argues it is inseparable from interpretation.

My research dives deeply into Nietzsche's concept of the will to power, a cornerstone of his view of human interpretation. He concludes his work *The Will to Power* with these striking lines: "This world is the will to power—and nothing besides! And even you yourselves are this will to power—and nothing besides!"[11]

I make sense of the will to power by thinking back to the good ol' days—or at least imagining them. I must've been eight or nine, spending the summer with my cousins on the shore of Lake Superior. One year, there was a sandcastle competition to determine who could build the "best" one. We leaped at the chance, determined to prove we were the greatest, coolest, most unstoppable sandcastle builders in all of Michigan.

Even then, that drive to shape something—impressive, meaningful, yours—was already there. That, I think now, was the will to power.

Almost immediately, we disagreed. I wanted to build the tallest tower. One cousin wanted to build a castle with a bridge and a moat that brought water in from the lake. Another cousin was obsessed with detail, wanting to build a small, intricate castle. Even as kids, we each valued something different: I valued scale, one valued engineering, and the other artistry and precision.

Those values shaped our interpretation of the sandcastle competition. They defined what we thought "best" meant and how to win.

For Nietzsche, this is how life works: A person's values shape their interpretation of the world, and both influence their will to shape it according to their vision.

So we each built our own. Mine stretched toward the sky like the Empire State Building. My cousin's had drawbridges and tunnels, a little Edinburgh castle. The third cousin's looked like a miniature cathedral; he even tried to mimic the Duomo's delicate spires.

When the competition ended, we wandered along the beach and saw that others had built similar castles—some tall, others ornate; one even had a fountain.

What a letdown.

We didn't feel so powerful anymore.

After the judges walked the beach, they couldn't decide on the best. There was just too much variation!

Looking back, I realize it was a competition of values. How can one determine which values create the best sandcastle?

The judges finally declared, "Good job, everyone!" and that was it. No one was declared the winner.

It was crushing.

And that's when it hit me—that sinking disappointment. The values of size, engineering, and intricacy had become equal, and uniqueness vanished. No one knew which sandcastle was more meaningful. Every sandcastle was just another sandcastle, and none of them really mattered anymore.

Eventually, the water came in and washed them all away.

That feeling, the emptiness of all of our effort, it all feels eerily similar to the despair I feel in Novemberton. Like no matter what the people in this town build or how hard they work, it all gets washed away. It's all pointless.

My trip to the beach illustrates what Nietzsche deduced about values: "Therefore, all the values which have previously rendered the world worthy of our esteem ultimately render it worthless when they prove inapplicable . . . all these values are the products of specific perspectives which proved useful for maintaining and increasing the power of specific forms of domination, perspectives which we have falsely projected into the nature of things."[12]

Values shape our interpretations and guide our actions, but in the end, they're subjective and ever changing. What once seemed meaningful can quickly lose significance, and no single value can claim universal superiority. Ultimately, values are fluid, and what we create or value can be swept away, leaving us to question its true meaning. This leads to a sense of meaninglessness and despair, as it becomes impossible to say what anything truly is if we are just interpreters, enacting values that shape life according to our desires.

I realize that Nietzsche's observation is the final bullet that killed God. It strips away any claim to ultimate meaning and exposes a world where values are subjective, shaped by the individual.

As society advanced in science and shifted in perspective, people began to realize that their ideas about God weren't grounded in divine truth, ideal forms, or an objective, rational self. Their ideas and beliefs were simply interpretations of the world—interpretations that everyone holds and that everyone uses to shape the world as they think it should be.

Thus, the madman enters the market and cries "God is dead." What, now, can claim ultimate meaning or divinity?

It is like a bad dream, one where every door leads back to the beginning, where the answer is always just out of reach. I see the line. From the ancient Israelites who walked with Yahweh, to the Platonists who glimpsed eternal forms, to the scientists who recentered the heavens, to the philosophers who placed human reason on the throne. God was once enthroned as a source that provided humankind with salvation and meaning.

And eventually, God was placed on trial, forced to explain himself in human terms. The verdict: not guilty, but irrelevant. Reason became king. Until even reason turned out to be unstable, just another interpretation among millions. And if everything is interpretation, then meaning isn't lost, it's impossible.

I return the books, open the door, and the wind cuts sharply against my skin. Novemberton breathes again, and I feel it swallow me whole.

KEEP SCROLLING

My gaze catches on a pile of sodden leaves near a decayed building. I feel it rising in me; this feels hopeless. What can present itself as the highest value? Who is the true God? Where is the perfect form or the objective self? How can I even know, if we're all just interpreters?

A memory pulls at me. The woman from the café. Her scrolling, her endless search. She did not know what she was looking for. The words rise unbidden: Maybe there is nothing to find.

Every voice on her screen—preachers, philosophers, self-proclaimed prophets—offering values, offering meaning. And yet they are all the same, shifting and crumbling under scrutiny, just interpretations masquerading as truth. Sandcastles against the surf.

A shiver crawls through me. Because in a world governed by science, where only the material is real, what ground is there to say otherwise?

I stop walking. It hits me all at once but feels like something I've known all along: The modern world has no answer, only the demand to search again tomorrow. A new value, a new interpretation.

I think of Nietzsche's warning. That nihilism isn't the absence of belief but the awareness of its impossibility. The recognition that no value is ultimate, no truth unshakable. I shudder. Because there are only two paths: Be consumed by the death of God or become your own god.

Both prospects chill me to the core.

Nihilism is the ghost at the feast. And it lingers still.

— Chapter Three —

THE GHOST AT THE FEAST

We are the hollow men
We are the stuffed men
Leaning together
Headpiece filled with straw. Alas!
Our dried voices, when
We whisper together
Are quiet and meaningless
As wind in dry grass
Or rats' feet over broken glass
In our dry cellar
Shape without form, shade without color
Paralyzed force, gesture without motion;
Those who have crossed
With direct eyes, to death's other Kingdom
Remember us—if at all—not as lost
Violent souls, but only
As the hollow men
The stuffed men.

—T. S. Eliot, "The Hollow Men"

The Hollow Man is no refuge.

Although it's only sometime after lunch, the pallor of the November sky seems to have closed upon the town, cloaking it in fog.

Lost in thought, I drift into a pub down the street. The table is sticky, voices low. The hum of people and smell of stale food pull to the surface a hunger I hadn't noticed, buried beneath the weight of old books and the cold realization that meaning itself had begun to rot long before I arrived.

I scan the menu, drawn to the block of text on the back. Since 1930, the pub has stood. A place built in the shadow of World War I; its name borrowed from Eliot's "The Hollow Men." The poem itself hangs on the wall near the pool table.

Like much of Europe, Eliot was shattered by the war. While the modern era promised progress and human achievement, it also produced a conflict that claimed around 20 million lives. Eliot believed that the modern world, the one Nietzsche's madman cried out in, had abandoned its moral and ethical values.

I glance up. There it is, in the dim corner of the bar. Framed and untouched.

> Our dried voices, when
> We whisper together
> Are quiet and meaningless
> As wind in dry grass
> Or rats' feet over broken glass
> In our dry cellar[1]

Ultimately, words carry no more lasting significance than breath exhaled in the cold. The clink of glasses, the murmur of conversation. The town's inhabitants engaged in their rituals—scrolling, laughing, drinking. In a pub named after "The Hollow Men," people gather together just the same.

Do they know?

Do they know that these things don't contain ultimate significance? That the words they speak are as empty and senseless as the wind?

I'm reminded of a time in my own life when I sat with my friend Sarah in a pub much like The Hollow Man. After laughs, jokes, and even a serious discussion, Sarah drifted into her phone. I wondered what she was feeling. I asked, "Do you ever think about what all *this* ultimately means?" Her response was a surrender: "I prefer to stay distracted so I don't have to."

The waitress scribbles down my order, avoids my eyes, and disappears with quiet relief. Two men debate last night's game; a woman at the far table fixes her lipstick using the camera on her phone; a student in the corner writes furiously in a notebook. A hungry curiosity takes root. Are these routines just routines? Or are they defenses, barriers built to hold back something darker?

I glance toward Eliot's poem again. It hasn't moved. But it feels closer now. Like Banquo's ghost watching Macbeth at his doomed feast.

> Avaunt, and quit my sight!
> Let the earth hide thee!
> Thy bones are marrowless, thy blood is cold.
> Thou hast no speculation in those eyes
> Which thou dost glare with![2]

I grip my glass tighter. Nihilism is the ghost at the feast. A presence everyone pretends not to see but one that lingers all the same.

INTERLUDE: A CLASS IN NIHILISM

In my university class on nihilism, I settle two things from the start. First, nihilism is the recognition that nothing—no belief, no value—holds ultimate meaning. Second, nothing kills a first date faster than mentioning it. To test this hypothesis, I have two students simulate an AI date where one person goes full Ecclesiastes. It usually ends up something like this:

(Scene: Dimly lit café, rain tapping against the window panes)

Lucia: "This place is nice. Feels cozy."

Frank: (sipping coffee) "Yeah. Cozy, like the calm before the void swallows us all."

Lucia: (laughs uneasily) "Um, what?"

Frank: "Ecclesiastes says it best: 'All is vanity.' Nothing we do matters. It's all just dust in the wind."

Lucia: (shifting) "Okay . . . but don't you think there's beauty in the little things?"

Frank: (leans closer, voice low) "Beauty is just a fleeting distraction from the abyss. One day, we'll all die and be forgotten."

Lucia: (stands abruptly) "I think I left my umbrella outside."

Frank: "The rain will wash it away . . . like everything else."

(Lucia backs away as Frank stares into his coffee. The rain outside intensifies.)

We call him Black Pill Frank. And every year, my students laugh. But the laughter is uneasy, the way people laugh when they recognize something uncomfortably true. Because there's a second, unspoken takeaway: He might be right.

WHEN THE GHOST WON'T BE IGNORED

Whether you are Frank or Lucia, there are times when the ghost at the feast cannot be ignored, when no distraction suffices. I've felt it myself. In the hospital corridor, in the chapel, in the moment before the news you don't want arrives. The ghost doesn't announce itself. It listens and waits. And eventually, it comes for everyone, whether through sorrow, silence, or sheer absurdity.

I've come to believe there are two moments when the ghost becomes impossible to ignore:

1. *When tragedy strikes and grief cannot be reconciled.* The suffering of the innocent causes everyone to pause, if only momentarily: natural disasters, school shootings, genocide, tragic car accidents. There are moments of silence after such tragedies—not beautiful but haunting, whispering in the hollow spaces where distractions once lived. In that stillness, doesn't the universe feel indifferent? How quickly our thoughts turn to question God. In these moments, no distraction is big enough to ignore the ghost who wails that the world is alone. And if the world is alone, without God, suffering is just suffering, void of meaning or redemption.
2. *When science confronts you with the smallness of human life.* Since the Scientific Revolution, the world has become increasingly aware of itself and its place among the stars. As knowledge has expanded, humankind's opinion of itself within the cosmos has diminished. Needing a break from my thoughts, I turn to my phone. As I swipe, a virtual tour of the universe unfolds on my screen. AI takes me from the dim corner of the pub to the farthest reaches of space, 46.5 billion light-years away. In all that vastness, at least two trillion galaxies, each with solar systems and planets, stretch out. While the universe appears to follow some kind of order, the chaos can't be ignored. As science presents its evidence for order, the ghost presses its case: Life is insignificant. How could it be anything more than stardust? It's a hard thought to ignore when the James

Webb Space Telescope captures the birth of stars in the shadows of black holes.

The ghost of nihilism does not announce itself with a scream. It settles in the bones, in the edges of thought. It waits, creeping in at the right moment.

THE TWO FACES

I finish my drink and glance toward the window. Fog presses against the glass with almost unnatural weight. And in that pressure, a realization: If all of this, every word, every ritual, is just a way to keep nihilism at bay, what happens when the illusion cracks?

It's everywhere in this town. And the reactions fall into two camps.

1. Meh-ism

"Meh-ism" is passively surrendering to life's lack of meaning and muttering "whatever" while going through the motions of life. Too tired to rage, too apathetic to care. Nothing is impressive. Nothing is beautiful. Nothing is worth doing. If nihilism is a truck, meh-ism is lying down in front of it and letting it flatten you like a Looney Tunes character, then waiting for it to back up and do it again.

This is what Nietzsche called "passive nihilism"—the weary resignation that meaning is dead and there's nothing left to do but shrug. No one openly admits to being a meh-ist. I've asked students in my philosophy classes if they know anyone who openly proclaims that they live without hope. It's always crickets—because who's going to say, "Yep, that's me! A human shrug in the shape of a person."

Yet we've all seen them. They're the ones who show up to a garden wedding in a Slipknot T-shirt and black half-pipe jeans because "love is meaningless, dude." But they aren't always dressed like they've just left a mosh pit. Sometimes they slip into designer outfits, sit on talk shows, and smile blankly, like Andy Warhol churning out copies of copies long after the meaning had faded. It's not an "f-you" to the system but a surrender. These are the ones succumbing to passive nihilism, worn down by the monotonous merry-go-round of life. Their souls are stuck in November's gloom. Meh-ists aren't claiming freedom or pursuing empowerment. They're just too exhausted to care.

2. Vibrant Voidism

"Vibrant voidism" is nihilism with a pulse. This type gets it: There's no ultimate meaning without immortality, but that doesn't mean the present is worthless. Sure, eternity is off the table, but the here and now? That's something.

Nietzsche called this "active nihilism"—a response to the death of meaning that ends not in despair but in defiance.[3] Active nihilists don't surrender like the meh-ists. They accept that values are human inventions, and they set out to create their own. This is their will to power: not just the will to survive the day-to-day but a drive to shape reality itself. They don't usually call themselves voidists—too dramatic—but they understand the stakes. Without meaning, life corrodes into passive nihilism, and that's insufferable.

One vibrant voidist who captured this tension was David Foster Wallace. His 2005 Kenyon College commencement speech offered a blunt map for navigating life's monotony without losing yourself. Wallace didn't give graduates the usual pep talk. Instead, he laid out the reality waiting for them:

> At the end of the day you're tired and somewhat stressed and all you want is to go eat . . . but then you remember there's no food at home . . . so now you have to get in your car and drive to the supermarket. It's the end of the work day and traffic is apt to be very bad. So getting to the store takes way longer than it should, and when you finally get there, the

> supermarket is crowded, because of course it's the time of the day when all the other people with jobs also try to squeeze in some grocery shopping. And the store is hideously lit and infused with soul-killing muzak . . . You have to wander all over the . . . confusing aisles . . . Then you have to take your creepy flimsy, plastic bags of groceries in your cart with the one crazy wheel that pulls maddeningly to the left, all the way out through the crowded, bumpy, littery parking lot. Everyone here has done this, of course. But it hasn't been part of your graduates' actual life routine, day after week after month after year. But it will be.

Wallace nailed it. Grocery shopping after work is a slow spiral through sameness, the endless slog that almost makes you want to quit right there in aisle five while hunting for watery Ragu to top your spaghetti.

But he didn't stop at describing the grind. He warned against the rot of meh-ism. Real survival, he argued, comes from training yourself to shape your thoughts, to choose what you pay attention to, to build dignity from the mundane: "If I don't make a conscious decision about how to think and what to pay attention to, I'm gonna be pissed and miserable every time I have to food-shop . . . The thing is that . . . there are obviously different ways to think about these kinds of situations."[4]

You can remain a hollow man or a hollow woman, or you can choose to fill the emptiness with meaning. Not cosmic, eternal meaning but enough to make the merry-go-round a life worth living.

That's all one can do in a world without God, where nothing transcendent remains beyond the closed system Novemberton is trapped in. Some give up. Some fight back. That's the shape nihilism takes. And in Novemberton, you can see both playing out, post by post, face by face.

So what gives rise to meh-ism and voidism? Beneath these reactions lies something deeper.

THE FIVE WHISPERS

A belief structure. A quiet architecture of assumptions. Five whispers echo beneath modern life:

1. *The universe is self-sustained. Science tells us that what we can observe is all there is—matter following laws, no miracles. Philosophers use the term "closed system" to refer to a universe that operates solely by its own rules, with no help from the outside. Humanist Manifesto II sums it up: "We find insufficient evidence for belief in the existence of the supernatural."*[5] *Every event is just a result of cause and effect—no divine intervention, no fate, no karma, no destiny. It's all matter acting upon matter in a chain of actions. The universe doesn't have a higher power keeping it running; physics is all that matters.*
2. *Everyone is mortal.* Nothing exists outside of the system—not you, not me, not the pub patrons. Sure, humans are unique in their intelligence and self-awareness, but that only makes us fancy stardust. When we die, our matter gets recycled, and the "person" we once were, vanishes. *Humanist Manifesto II* puts it bluntly: "As far as we know, the total personality is a function of the biological organism transacting in a social and cultural context. There is no credible evidence that life survives the death of the body."[6] That's the hard, cold truth of a closed system—too much to think about, let alone bring up on a first date.
3. *Everything is subjective.* In a closed system, matter itself has no meaning; it simply exists. Meaning isn't revealed from above, it's created from below. It's not divine revelation or cosmic truth, it's intelligent matter forming patterns. How we make that meaning depends on who we are, where we are, and, let's face

it, what's in it for us. It's a matter of personal perspective and self-interest. Consider a rainy day: A farmer understands it as an answered prayer. Perhaps he even thinks it's because he went to church last week. A bride sees punishment or neglect. Perhaps this rainy day is a result of her sin. A poet looks at the rain as inspiration, something beautiful to emulate in pen. Three interpretations. Three meanings. And the rain? Is rain.

4. *We can figure it out ourselves.* Relativism says that truth, morality, and meaning depend on culture, history, and society. Should you eat with a fork, or with your hands? Bow, or shake hands? Order a pork chop, or nah? It all depends. But what about universally bad stuff like murder and other heinous crimes? Baron d'Holbach, an Enlightenment thinker, argued that humans don't need God or an authoritative religious text to figure that stuff out. His version of ethics? "Use common sense to figure it out, people! Think about what works for humans to get along and flourish. And do that."[7] Essentially, ethics is humans negotiating how to get along with one another and how to survive and thrive. No need for outside input, just a bit of critical thinking and human cooperation.
5. *Life is absurd.* Humans have the ability to transcend themselves and recognize the inherent plight of their existence. We are, after all, thinking stardust. Have you ever envied a cat? Watched it chill in a patch of sunlight, utterly content, and felt a pang of jealousy? Not because you don't want to work but because the cat simply is. Cats don't wrestle with the purpose of life or their place in the universe. Meanwhile, like the preacher in Ecclesiastes, we lament life's insignificance, even as we still chase wealth, success, and self-agency. Oh, the grief. The bitter absurdity!

THE COLLAPSE: FOUR REACTIONS IN NOVEMBERTON

I look around the bar again. Almost everyone is tethered to their devices, their faces bathed in the halos of their screens. Conversation seems like a relic in this town. Not that I mind; after a long day already, my brain is saturated. A break is in order.

I turn to my phone. Why not check whether Novemberton has its own geotag? A bit of cultural research feels fitting. Maybe scrolling through the local posts will reveal how people have reacted to the ghost.

Their reactions fall into one of four groups:

1. Emotional Checkout

Passive nihilism rarely looks dramatic. It's not rage, it's a slow decay. When meaning collapses, so does motivation. The lack of passion on social media hits me in the face like a soggy newspaper.

Low-res images with disastrous editing and chaotic designs make dismal posts feel on-brand—the aesthetic of apathy. The content? Lifeless. There's the meme "I've got that dog in me," with a picture of a dog asleep on top of a pile of damp pizza boxes. Or the text exchange where a guy sends his grandpa a picture of his newborn—"Meet your new grandson!"—and the grandpa replies with a photo of his lunch: a sad grilled cheese on a paper plate. Then there's that one meme so dark it's practically a void. An elaborate birthday cake with candles topped off by shaky writing that reads, "One less year alive."

Demotivation is a vibe. The key word here is indifference—a catastrophic failure of attachment to anything remotely meaningful. Heck, you can't even muster excitement over a new grandson. It makes me think of that professor who described nihilism as "erectile dysfunction of the soul." Nothing turns you on anymore. Not even pretending.

I think of the Laodiceans. Jesus wasn't impressed with them in Revelation 3. He called them "lukewarm" and said that they were "wretched and miserable and poor and blind and naked" (Rev. 3:15–17 NLT). Notice all those ands? It's an emotional crescendo, a full-on roast. The Laodicean church is the poster child for passive nihilism. They weren't miserable because they lacked food or shelter, they were miserable because they had checked out emotionally. They are the textbook case of how loss of meaning goes hand in hand with apathy and despair.

2. Mental Freefall

Not all passive nihilism looks like apathy. Sometimes it looks like collapse. In Novemberton, social media feels like a village sport in mental freefall. Those who aren't checked out are spiraling, paralyzed by endless information with nowhere to land.

Oh, sure, there's some good on social media. But it can't compete with the never-ending stream of negative news and sensationalized headlines. You scroll past one catastrophe after another: a new flu virus, political meltdown, microplastics causing cancer, and, somewhere in there, someone's grandma's funeral livestream.

For those hovering on the edge, conspiracy theories offer a buffet of sorts: the earth is flat, aliens are launching drone attacks (obviously), and chemtrails are slowly killing us. Logging off is the best wellness tip out there, but this town is addicted, fully aware it's driving them nuts.

It's not that people believe everything, it's that the digital whiplash never stops. And when it snaps too hard, they turn to pills. Numbness is cheaper than clarity. Big pharma has that covered, but then again, they are the ones running the show. Each pop of the pill is just another small victory for the elites. The freefall continues, no bottom in sight.

3. "Screw It" Mode

This is the unfiltered, "I couldn't care less" vibe that dominates the feed. It's passive nihilism with a snicker.

These posts get all the love because they're as relatable as h-e-double-hockey-sticks.

Picture the perfect Parisian shot: a crisp baguette, an overpriced hotel, a view of Tour Eiffel. Cringe. No one believes in the curated dream anymore. Life isn't a cabana in the Maldives, it's a dumpster fire behind Taco Bell, and the only sane response is to laugh.

So they embrace the absurd. "I can't be bothered" selfies in a messy room of their overpriced dingy apartments. Stories about the impromptu Zyn runs to 7-Eleven. Plans? Overrated. Life isn't the American dream anymore. Why fight the inevitable when you can binge *Euphoria* and inhale five-dollar Kroger sushi every night? At least that's real.

It's a hollow pride that turns resignation into a virtue and calls it realism. You could even call it "numbed realism." This isn't rebellion, it's surrender dressed in sarcasm. Passive nihilism soundtracked by grunge guitars and memes.

It's not that these people are trying to burn it all down. They've just decided it's already ashes, so what's the point in pretending otherwise?

4. Raze Craze

Like any town, Novemberton has its political convictions, and boy, some people *love* sharing them—loudly and with all the grace of a wrecking ball. It's a digital cage match: both sides locked in a never-ending battle of demonizing the other. One side screeches about oligarchs, the other rages about socialists and communists, and both are convinced they're saving the world by slinging insults like confetti at a toxic wedding.

It's impressive how everyone has solved the world's problems: It's *them*. Words like *racist*, *oppressor*, and *elite* get tossed around freely. Everyone is yelling because, apparently, silence equals consent. If you aren't screaming your opinions into the void, you're a coward with zero conviction. And if you haven't picked a side? You're pathetic.

Watching it all unfold, post after post, reel after reel, I'm left feeling less than human.

The whole thing brings Nietzsche back to my mind. He said that in a nihilistic culture, "one actually puts one's shoulder to the plow and destroys."

It fits. In Novemberton, some don't surrender to despair, they fight back. But not with questions or quiet resolve. With flamethrowers, with rage, and with truth claims sharpened into weapons. That's active nihilism: the will to power untethered, unleashed on anyone who disagrees. They refuse to be hollow men. They want to matter.

And then there are the others, the ones who've already given up. The ones orbiting in numb resignation, scrolling, medicated, or muttering "whatever." That's passive nihilism: a slow fade into silence.

Two sides of the same coin. Without higher meaning to guide them, collapse and combustion become the only responses left.

ROUND AND ROUND THE PRICKLY PEAR

I sigh and put my phone down. I can't bear another second of Novemberton's digital despair.

"Check, please."

My eyes drift, almost reflexively, back to the menu. T. S. Eliot's lines wait there, patient, unmoved:

> Here we go round the prickly pear
> Prickly pear prickly pear
> Here we go round the prickly pear
> At five o'clock in the morning.

A children's rhyme, stripped of its innocence.

Then, so faint that I almost doubt it, I hear the echo of children singing. It's the kind of awareness that visits only in nightmares, and the low, looping monotony of background noise confirms it. They drink; they laugh; they fall in love. But it's all rehearsed, a mechanical carousel, a pantomime played out beneath dead light. A ritual not to find meaning but to forget its absence.

This prickly pear isn't a game. It's the rhythm of existence: meaningless, repetitive, and absurd. In a world without God, life can be nothing but this—round and round, pricked by thorns, endlessly orbiting a hollow core.

I see it now. Novemberton is caught between these poles. They dance; they drink; they post; they rage. They still care, though their meanings have curdled into irony, into rot. Still, round and round they go, desperate to make it matter.

But how long until they stop? How long until they collapse into true, unflinching nihilism?

And when they do—what then?

—— Chapter Four ——

RISE OF THE MONSTERS AND TROLLS

The modern mind is in complete disarray. Knowledge has stretched itself to the point where neither the world nor our intelligence can find a foothold. It is a fact that we are suffering from nihilism.

—Albert Camus

I step outside The Hollow Man and damp air brushes my face, clearing my mind slightly. Time feels suspended here, hanging between one moment and the next like a half-formed thought. A flyer pinned to the pub window catches my eye:

The Principles for a Human Religion
University of Novemberton
Furman Hall, Room 204

My mind wanders back to the café—the anxious student near the counter, turning that flyer over and over. Its bold letters jump in my memory. There's something unsettling in the repetition, a pulsing presence that persists around me, quiet but unmistakable. Out on the street, my thoughts scatter in the noise and clutter.

Injured? Get the Justice You Deserve!

End Hunger. Support a Local Food Bank Today!

Divorce Doesn't Have to Be Hard. Let Us Guide You.

Taste the Future—Try the Impossible Burger Today!

Bright billboards scream in urgency, but none promise lasting solutions.

I cross the street. Protesters chant loudly outside the central bank, their signs hastily painted: "STOP THE GREED!" I'm gripped by discomfort—what drives their conviction? I turn to my phone, scrolling habitually through news headlines:

MARKET DROPS 200 POINTS

STUDY WARNS OF RISING SEA LEVELS

ALGORITHM BEATS HUMANS IN
COMPLEX MEDICAL DIAGNOSIS

I recognize the impulse to escape, a small refuge from the noise, a familiar yet shameful retreat, making me no different from those around me who cling desperately to distraction. "There's no wifi in hell, but lots of hot spots!" breaks into my thoughts. A scorned preacher stands confidently holding a crude cardboard sign and shouts from the adjacent block. Teenagers jeer at him as they pass, their laughter ringing casually: "I'm waiting for the apocalypse! Heard it's gonna be lit!"

INFOBESITY

Novemberton's constant chatter is overwhelming—morality, data, technology, dilemmas, arguments, notifications, headlines, opinions, contradictions. A rotunda of noise, reminiscent of the suffocating library. Yet out on the street, it's worse: I cannot put the book down. Weary, I pause, recalling Ecclesiastes: "Of making many books there is no end, and much study wearies the body" (Eccl. 12:12).

Before today, I'd never understood this verse so clearly.

The preacher's observation about the toll of endless learning isn't just for scholars; it mirrors the human condition. Let's be honest: The exhaustion from scrolling endlessly is no different from the weariness that settles in after a long night lost in fruitless study.

Neil Postman, in his ominous introduction to *Amusing Ourselves to Death*, sets George Orwell's *1984* against Aldous Huxley's *Brave New World* as two differing visions of humanity's future relationship with information. Orwell feared censorship—a world where books would be banned. Huxley envisioned the opposite: a flood of information so vast that no one would bother to read a book—not deeply, at least. Orwell worried about scarcity. Huxley feared irrelevance.[1] As I navigate toward the university, Huxley's prediction looms larger than ever. I'm drowning in a constant stream of knowledge, overstimulated and exhausted—the weariness Ecclesiastes warned about.

Huxley wrote *Brave New World* at modernism's peak, not long after Nietzsche's madman declared the death of God. During the same time, society was realizing an affliction that now seems ominously related to God's demise: infobesity. Infobesity is just information overload—a mental buffet where you pile your plate high with endless servings of data and information, only to find your brain too stuffed to digest any of it. That concern was already evident as early as 1852, long before the telegraph, telephone, radio, or anything remotely resembling the internet.

In 1948, infobesity was finally acknowledged as a problem at the Royal Society's scientific information conference. That accounted only for scientific data, never mind the feast of other kinds of information served up as telecommunications advanced. Unsurprisingly, the problem kept escalating, and by the 1990s, info gluttony had earned a new name: the "TMI effect"—because apparently too much information is more of a headache than a help.

During the twentieth century:

- A single weekly edition of the *New York Times* contained more information than the average seventeenth-century English person would have encountered in their entire lifetime.
- The English language had five times more words than Shakespeare ever had to work with.
- More information was produced in a few decades than in the previous five thousand years.
- Collections at major US research libraries doubled between 1876 and 1990.
- The number of publicly available records jumped from 52 million in 1972 to 5.3 billion by 1994.
- The number of documents on the internet doubled from 400 million to 800 million between 1998 and 2000—meaning it would take around 200,000 years to read the internet.[2]

All of this was achieved with dial-up! Oh yes, the good old days of dial-up. If you're a millennial, you certainly remember that screeching sound as your computer connected to the internet. You'd finally connect to AOL, just to find out that PrincessGurl23 was offline and Sk8rBoy007 was "brb." Fast-forward to today, and now we have smartphones, social media, cloud computing, Wi-Fi that doesn't cut out every five minutes, Starlink, streaming media, 5G, quantum computing, AR/VR worlds such as the metaverse, and AI such as ChatGPT and

Grok. And by the time you are finished reading this, something *new* will already be in the works that makes your current smartphone feel like you're holding a Discman. (Gen Z, you don't understand the pain of CD skippage.)

But let's really put this data boom into perspective. Ready?

Back in 1999, when you were munching on Funyuns and guzzling Surge (RIP), the world was home to around 0.025 zettabytes of data. Fast-forward to 2010, and that had exploded up to two zettabytes. By 2023, it was a whopping 120 zettabytes, and by 2024, it was 149. Think that's a lot? Just wait. In 2025, we're talking 181 zettabytes. And by 2028? Take a deep breath: 394 zettabytes.[3]

At this point, you're likely wondering, "What in the heck is a zettabyte?" Glad you asked. A zettabyte is a trillion gigs. So if you tried to store one zettabyte of information on DVDs (which would be the ultimate millennial nightmare), that stack would stretch to the moon and back one hundred times. And if you decided to watch that one zettabyte of data without pausing to go to the bathroom, take a nap, or warm up a delicious pepperoni and cheese Hot Pocket, you'd be watching for 50.7 million years.

But let's not stop there. It's 2028, and you want to binge-watch all 394 zettabytes of data on the internet. Hold on to your bucket hat: That would be more than twenty billion years of straight viewing. If you somehow did this while traveling at the speed of light, you'd make your way across a fourth of the observable universe. So yeah, we're talking a lot of data here, enough to fill a quarter of the universe. You may want to invest in a comfy chair.

DATA DREAD

Infobesity has given rise to a data drain—a freak-out when your brain finally says "enough." Picture your grandpa, polyester pants flapping after dinner, glaring at a slice of peach cobbler like it's one of the four horsemen of the apocalypse. "If I keep looking at that thing," he groans, "I'll need a therapist."

Bo Burnham, prophet of our digital demise, captures this meltdown in his singsong anthem "Welcome to the Internet." It starts off light and chipper, like a stroll through a candy store, but soon spirals into a full-blown horror show where innocent travel blogs and pasta tips mingle with tragic stories and bomb-making instructions.

The chorus sums it up: everything everywhere all at once. The sheer overload of content is not only distracting, it's disorienting. Boredom becomes a crime when constant content floods your life.

Burnham's song echoes the words of Albert Camus, the French-Algerian philosopher who warned, "The modern mind is in complete disarray. Knowledge has stretched itself to the point where neither the world nor our intelligence can find a foothold. It is a fact that we are suffering from nihilism."[4]

Camus, who died in 1960, long before this circus began, recognized that the rapid expansion of knowledge had outpaced society's ability to process it. Information was coming in so hot that it burned, leaving us flailing to piece together a coherent worldview.

When everything is available everywhere, all the time, information loses its value. It exhausts itself, making sifting through it feel pointless. It's not that nothing is coherent; it's that everything is coherent, and it's exhausting. There are too many ways to organize society, let alone our lives. How do we know which way is right?

Opinions clash with opinions. Commitments start flying out the window. One expert claims nicotine pouches cause cancer and liver failure; another insists they boost blood flow and offer revolutionary health benefits. One person swears the vegan lifestyle is our destiny, while another, looking as if he time-traveled from the Stone Age, insists our ancestors hunted dinosaurs and feasted on their carcasses. Then there's the doctor who says it doesn't matter what you eat, as long as it's within a four-hour window. You jump from diet to diet, boasting about your enlightenment at the gym, until the chaos of conflicting ideas drags you into dietary nihilism. All diets seem to make sense, so none of them do. No universal dietary truth exists; do what feels right. "I'll take a number one, please, with a Diet Coke!"

And it isn't just about diets. It extends to religions, theological stances, and political ideologies—a never-ending smorgasbord of ideas, each clashing with the next.

THE INTERNET HAS TURNED ON US

Modernity's relentless pursuit of information has buried us in noise and called it clarity. As I walk, I can't help but hear the ominous echoes of Tolkien's Lord of the Rings, reminding me of Sauron, once the gifted Maia Mairon, apprentice to Aulë the Smith, before his renowned craftsmanship became corrupted by power. It feels like a warning: We've made incredible technological advancements, but even our finest creations, like his, can twist into destructive forces.

Consider the atom: a monumental discovery that eventually unleashed nuclear bombs in 1945. Think of painkillers: lifesaving for managing chronic pain, yet now fueling an opioid crisis. And then there's AI. Imagine a "smart" robot without feelings, armed with an assault rifle, or robots that become the object of darker, twisted desires. The internet connects the world, opens opportunities, and democratizes education, but it also shortens our attention spans, fuels online addiction, spreads misinformation, and traps us in echo chambers where radical ideas flourish.

AI and the internet have become the Agent Orange of the modern age—tools once created for good that now reveal their toxic side. Infobesity and data dread are just the tip of the iceberg. It's no wonder people try to log off, declaring, "I'm done with social media for a while" (even if it's only temporary).

We've forged our own monster, reminiscent of Skynet. As Elon Musk quips, "Please be kind to us, Chat."[5]

Ultimately, while technology has given us access to countless truths, it has also birthed a post-truth world where any outrageous claim can be googled and seemingly validated. The frantic search for meaning only amplifies our collective sense of meaninglessness.

BORING

The cold grows sharper. I sink into my coat and pull it around me tightly. A square opens ahead, its edges drawn by quiet cafés and subdued shops. One catches my eye, a window dressed in wool, tweed, and browns so deep they seem to hush the air around them. When I enter the store, the warmth is not immediate, but the silence is. No customers. No chatter.

I browse without urgency, grateful for the absence of small talk again. A mustard scarf—soft, warm, and unassuming—draws my attention. I take it to the counter, where the tailor sits behind a screen, unmoved by my presence.

When he looks up, his eyes are vacant, glassed over with that same dull stare I've seen all over town. I ask what he's watching. He shrugs. "Just scrolling," he says, with a vague wave toward the door. "Can you blame me?" I glance around. The quiet is stale, as if the very air has forgotten what it means to move. His words, though offhand, are understood. The town is buzzing with information and convenience, and yet everyone seems to be trying to escape it, fleeing into devices, distractions, anything to be elsewhere.

I realize the tailor is simply bored. Not in the way a child is bored on a rainy day, this is the boredom that comes when even novelty loses its shape. The kind of boredom that arises only when everything is available, yet nothing satisfies. The line between significance and noise has blurred to the point of vanishing. In a world bloated with data, even the extraordinary becomes indistinct.

This is the new affliction: not ignorance but saturation. Apathy not from lack but from too much. Everything flattens.

Words from the book of James ring in my mind: "Such a person is double-minded and unstable in all they do" (James 1:8). It fits. The minds here, perhaps even mine, are tossed endlessly by the latest trend, the newest outrage, the next thing that might promise significance. A viral prank. A conspiracy. A fleeting answer to that hollow waiting-room sensation life seems to carry now. But nothing holds.

The tailor doesn't see it, not fully. But I do. His drifting curiosity isn't just habit, it's survival. It's all he has left.

I clutch the scarf and wrap it sharply around my neck as I step back into the biting cold of the town square.

Noah V. Emberton, first mayor of the town, immortalized in 1911 by his own order. I stare up at his statue. And something clicks. For a moment, I imagine someone standing beneath it at midnight, hoping luck might drip down like rain. According to the plaque, touching the peg leg brings life. The leg is worn smooth. I don't laugh.

People have always made idols. Objects to carry their hopes, soak up their longings. In older times, they carved them from stone and wood, bowed to them, left offerings. Now they build them in pixels and broadcasts, shrines of spectacle dressed as entertainment. A viral clip becomes a kind of altar. A trending figure, a temporary god. The statue, the sports star, the influencer—they promise not salvation but attention. And attention, in Novemberton, is the new favor of the gods.

They don't build cathedrals anymore. They build platforms. Streams. Feeds. Followers become worshipers. Algorithms become priests.

Athletes whack balls with sticks not for the love of the game but because billions are watching, hoping to borrow some of the glow. Every screen becomes a pulpit. Every post, a prayer. The rituals are new, but the longing is ancient.

With eight billion people brushing shoulders in cities too loud for meaning, the hunger grows louder still. And so they climb towers, livestream their lives, kneel before curated idols of their own making, hoping for luck or a glimpse of mattering.

I continue toward the university, the fog enveloping me, swallowing me whole. Somewhere between the zettabytes and the yawning dread, a conclusion forms. There are two ways people respond to the boredom now: They put their trust in monsters. Or they become trolls.

IN MONSTERS WE TRUST

I think again about the tailor—about his gaze, hollow and fixed, and how it mirrors others I've seen in Novemberton. Everyone staring into something: a screen, a mirror, a window. Waiting, perhaps, for life to clarify itself. But it doesn't. It scrolls. It loops. It drifts. Like a town long since untethered from its anchor.

There's a quiet horror to it. No tyrant, no disaster, just an ache without origin. Boredom with no beginning, no end. I understand now why people build monsters. Not the kind with claws or teeth but monsters of progress, of invention, of spectacle. Things large enough to distract, powerful enough to believe in. Technology, algorithms, social clout. Bodies reshaped by machines. Truth reshaped by votes. Anything that might rise above the gray and gesture toward the sublime, even if it devours us in the process.

Frankenstein surfaces in my mind. Not the film caricature but the young man in Mary Shelley's pages—brilliant, fevered, desperate to overcome death itself. Victor Frankenstein, the poster child for mad scientists everywhere, was driven by the death of his mother to unlock the secrets of nature. He wasn't just a regular scientist; no, he was a full-on, textbook obsessive. Dr. Frankenstein himself says, "It was the secrets of heaven and earth that I desired to learn; and whether it was the outward substance of things or the inner spirit of nature and the mysterious soul of man that occupied me, still my inquiries were to the metaphysical, or in its highest sense, the physical secrets of the world."[6]

He wasn't trying to be evil. He was trying to matter. And in a way, he succeeded. The monster lived. Not well. Not happily. But it lived.

Looking back, Frankenstein's regret reads like something straight out of Ecclesiastes—a lament for the weight of knowing too much. "Learn from me," he warns, "if not by my precepts, at least by my example, how dangerous is the acquirement of knowledge, and how much happier that man is who believes his native town to be the world, than he who aspires to become greater than his nature will allow."[7]

It's a quiet devastation, one I understand more now than when I first read it. Because in Novemberton, knowledge is not scarce. It floods. Overflows. Drowns. And in its wake, the ache remains.

So too in Novemberton, the monsters live: endless updates, new platforms, engineered breakthroughs. All of them stitched together from our deepest fear—not of dying but of having no purpose while we live. Monsters, yes. But better a monster than a void.

ENTER THE TROLLS

I pass another empty town square, one of many abandoned spaces in Novemberton. Town squares once buzzed with the life of bold proclamations and heated debates. My mind drifts back to the library, where Alexis de Tocqueville's voice lingered among the books, praising the vitality of public discourse. And to Søren Kierkegaard, the gloomy Danish philosopher, who was terrified and saw the town square as a grand stage for nihilism: "It is frightful that someone who is no one . . . can set any error into circulation with no thought of irresponsibility and with the aid of this dreadful disproportioned means of communication."[8]

Kierkegaard wasn't against free speech, he was afraid of boredom. And looking around, I realize he might have had a point. The town square, once a meaningful center of discourse, now resembles endless scrolling online—anonymous, self-assured crowds gathering to unleash their anger, anxiety, and boredom. It's less about seeking truth and more like venting in a public bathroom, flushing away responsibility.

It's trolling, essentially modern-day gladiators in a digital Colosseum entertaining bored, numb audiences. Kierkegaard could have been describing internet trolls when he wrote about countless apocalyptic prophecies filling idle lives: "In our times, when so little is done, an extraordinary number of prophecies, apocalypses, glances at and studies of the future appear, and there is nothing to do but join in and be one with the rest."[9] Everyone believes they're righteous; everyone believes they're fighting evil. But does any trolling battle truly settle the deep questions that anchor meaning?

No. The cycle continues because the dopamine hit from likes makes us feel falsely assured. The crowds remain restless, empty, and comfortably numb. In this online takeover, the high street and its squares fade away, replaced by nihilistic digital spectacles.

Up ahead, the university gates appear—iron and ivy bound. I pause, the cold gnawing at my knuckles, my scarf a little suffocating. I step toward Furman Hall, grateful for an escape from the cold. I pass a man smoking beneath a flickering streetlight. His eyes are red. His phone glows in his hand, but he's not touching it. Just watching. Waiting. For what, I don't know. Maybe he doesn't either. Perhaps this lecture will offer clarity; something meaningful might finally emerge, or perhaps it's just another cycle, another turn around the prickly pear.

Chapter Five

DARK CATECHISM

Now when everything out there is much more agonizing, there's also an unquitting desire to figure out meaning, you can't tear yourself away from Dostoyevsky, and it's amazing how much it seems it was written yesterday.

—N. Mering (writing to her teacher Ernest L. Radlov)

The lobby of the hall is abuzz with anticipation. Backpacks rustle as students scroll their phones and chat with one another and wait for the doors to the lecture to open. The smells of coffee, gum, and damp fabric hang in the air. I'm surprised that so many have shown up. The flyer hadn't promised anything exciting; "The Principles for a Human Religion" is hardly a rock concert. I'd expected apathy, but hardly a crowd.

The doors open after a few minutes, and we shuffle in. I take a seat near the door. The room is vast and semicircular with wooden seats in rows that slope down toward a stage of polished oak. There are a few empty seats here and there, but not many. At first glance, nothing here is overtly sinister, yet the air in the room feels unnatural and is sharp with something clinical and metallic. I glance around. The students don't look quite right. There's youth in their faces, yes, but also something aged. Their eyes seem tired in ways that don't belong to people so young, their postures slumped as if they've been doing heavy labor.

On the screen, announcements shuffle past: campus closures for federal holidays, a symposium on evolutionary biology at Murdock Hall, a critical thinking exposé at Heller Hall, a student union forum on genetic editing and human potential. A professor's book signing at Clack Library: *Morality and Theism Without Divine Command*.

It's not all academic. There's also a fundraiser for a war-torn country, a global food festival, and the Winter Solstice Ball, which seems to be generating real excitement. Finally, a slide about the University of Novemberton Excellence Award. It praises advancements in science, technology, and innovation "toward a better humanity."

From this stream of slides, I begin to sense the architecture of the town's belief system:

1. Humanity centralizes the sciences: Humans offer the framework for understanding and shaping the world.
2. Humanity determines morality: Ethics are crafted by humans alone.
3. Humanity controls its fate: The future is shaped by human will and innovation.
4. Humanity elevates humanity: Humans are revered for pushing the limits of their potential.

It all confirms what I've seen: that in Novemberton, humanity has become the highest authority. But if meaning must come from within, from our own will, then what happens when that will falters? If all meaning is an interpretation, then what governs the interpreter?

ELEVATING THE SELF

A Scripture passage rises in my mind, one that feels unnervingly apt: "But understand this . . . dangerous times [of great stress and trouble] will come [difficult days that will be hard to bear]. For people with be lovers of self [narcissistic, self-focused]" (2 Tim. 3:1–2 AMP).

These verses describe a society stripped of humility, loveless, self-obsessed, out of control. The original language calls it *philautos*, a people so enamored with themselves their enamorment turns to the worship of self. A society kissing its own reflection. It's as if the town, and perhaps all of us, have begun to believe our own myths—that we are the creators, the sustainers, the redeemers. And in doing so, we've replaced the divine with something brittle. Ourselves.

As my thoughts spiral, the lights dim. Four panelists step onto the stage, each claiming a seat in a sleek leather chair. A moderator follows, promising only to introduce and guide transitions. Then the names are given: the Hero, the Vanguard, the Thinker, and the Rebel.

The figures settle in, but something in the room shifts. The temperature doesn't drop, it withdraws. A kind of silence creeps in, as if people have forgotten to breathe.

And in that pause, my heart almost stops. I am not here to attend a lecture. I am here to watch the dead speak.

The Hero

The Hero immediately stands out. He's leaned back in his chair with relaxed shoulders, exuding an air of calm detachment and eerie focus, unmoved by the applause of the students or the moderator's awkward attempts at humor. His gaze drifts like he's watching a scene no one else can see. A tea set sits next to him, absurd for a dead man in a worn-out lecture hall. He handles it with ritualistic precision, each gesture so mechanical it seems like he's checking boxes in a ceremony he's performed before. As he raises the teacup to his lips, a thought slips into my mind, impossible to shake: I wonder whether dead men can taste tea.

That's when I notice it: His lips curl into a faint smirk. As if he heard me. As if he's in on something, and I'm not sure whether I'm supposed to laugh or shudder at the joke.

The moderator opens the floor for the Hero to speak on the principles of human religion, and the moment he begins, it becomes clear—strange as he may seem—that his words are far from the ramblings of a halfwit. If anything, his ideas are disturbingly well thought out.

He is obsessed with the notion that humans can and must become God. In a world without a deity, he argues, humanity must seize the role of lord over creation. Between slow, methodical sips, he introduces a concept he has long been working on: the man-God. The term strikes me as a deliberate inversion of the God-man—Jesus Christ. It's a reversal that thrusts humanity into the place Christ once held. As I try to grasp what it might mean for a human to be divine, he seems to anticipate the thought and offers an answer: Self-will is the essence of godhood. All former meaning—meaning that came from God—was just an illusion. Human will is the only reality.

With steady calm, he declares, "If God exists, then all will is his, and I can't escape his will."[1] He sweeps the room with his detached gaze. Then slowly sips his tea, the soft clink slicing the silence when he puts it down. "If he does not exist, then all will is mine, and I am obliged to proclaim self-will."[2]

He goes on to explain the logic of his man-God philosophy. For it to become a religion, he says, humanity must accept four things:

1. God is dead.
2. Humans are no longer bound by God.
3. Humans are governed only by their self-will.
4. Humanity's godlike self-will must be used to create a new world.

"When humans accept these terms," he proclaims, "then there will be a new life, a new man; everything will be new . . . then history will be divided into two parts: from the gorilla to the annihilation of God, and from the annihilation of God to the transformation of the earth."[3]

A new era for humanity.

He leans back in his chair as the audience sits frozen in silence. Even in a town that buried God long ago, something about his words feels . . . dangerous. Maybe it's the certainty. Maybe it's the quiet, mechanical way he speaks, as if he's already lived this out. Whatever it is, no one dares move. The moderator clears his throat, unsure how to proceed, and hesitantly asks him to elaborate on the idea of self-will.

He begins to tell his story—a life consumed by the pursuit of self-will. He speaks of his death with pride: a self-inflicted gunshot to the temple. Suicide. I squint and notice a scar I'd somehow missed. This man in front of me took his own life in an act of defiance, an attempt to become the first man-God. A man without limits. Without fear. Beyond death.

His suicide wasn't an act of surrender. It was a declaration of his divinity.

To prove that humanity can be God—*is* God—he had to show that nothing, not even death, could control him. His reasoning terrifies me.

What terrifies me even more is that he sees his death not as a tragedy but as a symbolic victory for all humanity. Through it, he believes he shattered the old order—where death ruled over man—and ushered in a new era. An era in which nothing can prevent humans from taking the place God once held. In his mind, his death confirmed what Nietzsche's madman had proclaimed: God is indeed dead. Humans can—and must—take his place. Nothing is stopping them.

As I scan the audience, I see faces fixed in shock, confusion, and disgust. But he remains unfazed—too deep in his logic, too convinced of its truth. While others see only madness, he believes he has achieved clarity. He's blind to the reality that his search for meaning devoured him from within and left him dead. He didn't die a hero. He died like a dog—in empty misery. His death didn't fill the void, it only revealed how deep it truly was. Self-will, without a foundation beyond the self, crumbles into a terrifying kind of nothingness.

My thoughts drift to 2 Timothy, again, and its warning of the chaos that comes when human beings exalt themselves and try to be gods.

To my relief, the other figures on the stage seem just as disturbed as the rest of us. All except one—a man with sharp, handsome features and undeniable magnetism. There's something commanding about him, something that sets him apart. Even the Hero seems to shrink in his presence.

As it turns out, these two men once knew each other.

The Vanguard

I notice that the Vanguard has maintained a composed posture throughout the hero's discourse. His hands rest lightly on the armrests, unmoved, yet taut with subtle tension, hinting at his intensity. At times, when the Hero speaks, he appears intrigued, perhaps even quietly fascinated, but is never stirred, never convinced. I find myself contemplating his striking features: jet-black hair, calm eyes, square jaw chiseled with perfect symmetry. It seems the beauty of a mask worn not to hide emotion but to erase it entirely. There's a coldness that makes his presence inhuman.

When the moderator opens the floor to him, I learn of his aristocratic lineage. Raised in privilege, he moved through life with an effortless air of superiority, idolized by those around him. People gravitated toward him, and in turn, he inspired them. His magnetism was both captivating and consuming. Over time, his influence over people elevated him to something near divinity.

Midway through the discussion, the Hero suddenly interrupts the Vanguard and exclaims, "Remember what you have meant in my life!"[4]

The moment shocks me. This isn't just a memory, it's a confession. Whatever history they share, it runs deep. I can sense that the Hero once admired and followed him.

Yet the Vanguard continues without acknowledging him. He tells the audience he was once called a man who knew nothing of fear. In a duel, he could stare down the barrel of a pistol with chilling indifference, aim, and kill, utterly untouched by the ordeal. For a moment, his power seduces the room. Then his eyes drift to me. I feel his gaze settle on me like a weight, as if he senses something different in me. But he moves on, untouched by the moment, adrift completely within himself.

Over time, his indifference deepened, morphing into cruelty. He tested it every chance he could, desperate to feel something—anything. He once twisted the nose of a harmless old man to see his reaction, passionately kissed another man's wife in public, and even bit the governor's ear. These weren't acts of impulse but experiments, desperate attempts to feel something. Yet each one left him unchanged, reinforcing his frozen November soul.

And while the Vanguard remains unconvinced of the Hero's philosophy of absolute self-will, it becomes obvious that he is its blueprint, the inspiration for the Hero's vision of the man-God.

But he, too, failed at achieving divinity.

He moved through a life of influence, performing gestures stripped of meaning, leaving only ruin in his path. No principle guided him, no cause ever took root. "But what to apply my strength to—that I've never seen, I don't even see it now."[5] As the embodiment of the so-called man-God, he scattered chaos with every step, a hollow force cloaked in power, until the emptiness he carried consumed him completely.

He recounts the story of his secret wife, who was mentally challenged and of much lower social standing. He married her not out of love or even pity but to mock social norms and assert his dominance. He was no husband. His radical pursuits placed her in harm's way, and she became collateral damage.

His apathy made him complicit in her murder. No mourning followed, only a deepening hollow.

He told of a friend, an ideological opponent, who was brutally murdered by a revolutionary group for a belief he had convinced him to adopt. The horror of it all was that he watched the plan unfold and did nothing to stop it. Silent. Unmoved. He let him die.

As his story unfolds, the connection between the Vanguard and the Hero is confirmed. As I began to suspect, he had encouraged the Hero's beliefs. His influence convinced him that suicide is the ultimate way to transcend human limitations and become divine. The Vanguard's manipulative words, fearless atheism, and rejection of morality contributed to the tragic spiral of a good man.

It is clear that the Vanguard is no savior at all. He ruins everyone he encounters. The coldness of his soul, a perpetual November, spreads quietly, leaving only devastation behind.

Eventually, that devastation turned inward. He speaks briefly of a fleeting encounter with a monk, a moment of spiritual introspection that flickered and died without leaving a mark. Not long after, they found him hanged, alone, in a tiny room. A man of charisma and power, who once reached for godhood, found himself confined to the smallest prison of all—his own mind.

His suicide letter unearthed a long-buried crime against a young girl—a crime so horrific he had concealed it not only from the world but from himself. The confession held no trace of remorse, only a final, unflinching descent into nihilism.

As I listen, a sickness settles in me—not shock but grief. A slow, sinking comprehension that defies reason, heavy and hard to name.

The Vanguard ends his monologue with a hollow admission: "I've tried my strength everywhere."[6] But like the Hero, he never became a god, only another man, consumed by the very self he sought to transcend.

His mask-like exterior—once striking, almost beautiful—now seems only a fitting facade for the detachment within. Beneath that polished stillness lies a cold, cavernous emptiness. And now, looking closer, I wonder whether it was always there. I notice just below his jaw, half shadowed and faint, a dark bruise circling his neck. He doesn't seem emotionless anymore, he seems haunted by demons.

With difficulty, I gather my thoughts:

1. Godlessness has led to the rejection of traditional morality.
2. Godlessness has fostered emptiness, cold indifference, and cruelty.
3. Godlessness has resulted in an unbearable abyss of meaning.
4. Godlessness has led to the failure of achieving divinity.

As I look around, I'm relieved I'm not the only one disturbed by the Vanguard's discourse. Perhaps no one feels it more deeply than the panelist known as the Thinker. He interrupts, unsolicited by the moderator, with a sharp remark: "But don't you see? You speak of your indifference, but your entire life has been a search for meaning, an attempt to escape the cold November of your soul. You are not indifferent, you are terrified. And now, so am I. And now, so are we."

The Thinker

I had noticed the Thinker from the start. He'd been engaged throughout, sitting with one leg crossed over the other. He leaned back as if at ease, but his fingers tapped the armrest, signaling a growing frustration. An impatience that finally surfaced with his interruption—he had reached his breaking point.

As he takes over the discussion, his intellectual brilliance becomes clear. He isn't just smart but a natural talent. His raw ability has been honed in rigorous academic environments, making him skilled in both science and philosophy.

I begin to understand that the Vanguard's life serves as the perfect example of the Thinker's philosophical dilemma—likely the very reason he's interrupted him.

On one hand, the Thinker cannot believe in God, especially because of the suffering of innocent children.

He recalls a story he had heard about a five-year-old girl who wet her bed. Her parents locked her in an outhouse during the winter, and she got frostbite. When she tried to escape, they smeared her face with her own excrement.

He also tells about a young boy who accidentally hurt his father's hunting dog while throwing a rock. The boy's father unleashed the dog on him and watched indifferently as it mauled his son.

How can a good God allow such suffering?

The Thinker concludes, "If everyone must suffer in order to buy eternal harmony with their suffering, tell me what children have to do with it. It's quite incomprehensible why they should have to suffer . . . If the suffering of children goes to make up the sum of suffering needed to buy truth, then I assert beforehand that the whole of truth is not worth such a price."[7]

If this life's suffering is supposed to promise happiness in the next, he refuses to accept it.

"We can't afford to pay so much for admission. And therefore I hasten to return my ticket."[8]

He shares a theological parable he once told his brother—about divine love, human suffering, and free will—which reinforced his belief that a benevolent, omnipotent God does not exist.

On the other hand, the Thinker is terrified of a world without God and the implications it brings. He finds it just as difficult to accept a world with God as one without God. A world without God means no meaning and no objective morality. "Without God, everything is permitted."

While he denounces the actions of the Vanguard, he struggles to understand why the Vanguard shouldn't act the way he does. Without God, where can one find an objective moral framework? It might be, as Nietzsche suggested, that morality is shaped by interpretation and the will to power, and this realization unsettles the Thinker deeply.

It's clear that the Thinker is uncomfortable with his lack of faith. He has always been uneasy. He longs to find God, but he cannot arrive at this conclusion through reason or abstract thought.

He opens up further, speaking about the murder of his father. His father was corrupt—unrestrained and promiscuous, neglectful ofhis children. As a rational man, the Thinker could not understand his father's immoral lifestyle and despised him for it. There were times when he had even wished his father dead. But, being a man of logic, he knew this was wrong. Eventually, his half brother killed their father.

The murder unsettled the Thinker, plunging him into depression and unbearable guilt. He began hallucinating, unraveling under the thought that he was indirectly responsible for the murder. He was tormented by the thought that his rejection of God and belief in moral relativism had influenced his half brother to commit the murder. While he had once claimed that without God, everything is permissible, the murder forced him to confront the reality of moral wrongdoing. His depression and guilt seemed to confirm that he had violated a deeper moral order. The inner conflict shook the foundation of his beliefs.

He recalls a terrifying moment when the devil himself appeared and mocked his beliefs. The Thinker had once surmised that renouncing God would lead humankind to titanic pride, where human will and science would triumph. He envisioned a future where humankind would accept death "proudly and calmly, like a god."[9] Yet in the presence of the devil's ridicule—a presence I realized was the product of his psychological collapse—the Thinker realized that such a vision of the future could not come so benignly. His intellect, which had once been his pride, was now his ruin. Perhaps the collapse of his rationality signaled that something deeper was taking hold. But there was no way to know.

After hearing his struggle, I was left with four key takeaways:

1. On the one hand, innocent suffering makes the existence of a benevolent God seem impossible.
2. On the other hand, without a benevolent God, objective morality dissolves and everything becomes permissible.
3. Our conscience resists the freedom to act without moral constraints.
4. Doing whatever you feel is right brings not freedom but guilt, emptiness, intensifying the struggle for meaning.

As the Thinker winds down, I'm sure I hear him mutter, "I am a scoundrel." I glance around, wondering whether anyone else has heard it. But before I can react, the Rebel begins to speak.

The Rebel

The Rebel is disheveled. His trousers are wrinkled and mismatched with his linen shirt. His face is gaunt, pale, and marked by dark bags beneath his eyes. While the others spoke, I noticed how he kept his gaze low, withdrawn, weighed down by some invisible burden. Every so often, his jaw would clench, his teeth grinding, as if trying to suppress an anxiety he carried inside.

He must have heard the Thinker's comment about being a scoundrel, because without any prompt from the moderator, he launches into his discourse, saying, "I was a louse—no, worse. I thought I was extraordinary, above them all. But I was nothing. I was filth."

Sweat forms on his forehead, and his words grow erratic,

disjointed, his voice rising with intensity: "The truth is, I'm more vile than the louse I killed because, yes, maybe she was worthless, a parasite on society. But I killed her. I killed her and her sister to prove a theory."

The room reacts with a collective gasp.

He begins to recount his life.

He had grown up with a mother and a sister, both of whom had placed their hopes in him. His mother believed he was exceptional, destined for greatness. As he moved away from traditional beliefs, his ideas grew more radical, and his inner torment deepened. His philosophy centered on the idea of "the extraordinary man"—someone above ordinary morality who could cast aside traditional ethics for the greater good. Those who didn't meet that standard, the "ordinary" people, were to him nothing more than "lice," insignificant and disposable.

According to his thinking, the extraordinary man had the right to break moral laws if doing so served a higher purpose, even if it meant wading through blood.

His hero was Napoleon, someone he believed had transcended morality by creating something new, even at the cost of violence and death.

"In creating a new law, he broke the old one, handed down for generations and held sacred by the people. He did not shrink bloodshed," the Rebel explains.[10]

The extraordinary individual's conscience, he believed, would not be burdened by guilt or remorse so long as the ends justified the means.

His own increasing poverty and radical ideas led him to target a woman he viewed as a parasite—a pawnbroker who exploited the poor while living comfortably. He had overheard someone suggest that taking her life and redistributing her wealth could be justified.

"What do you think, would not one tiny crime be wiped out by thousands of good deeds? One death and a hundred lives in exchange—it's the most basic arithmetic!"[11]

He didn't see this as a coincidence but as confirmation. He

believed that as an extraordinary man, he was meant to act, meant to kill the pawnbroker for the good of society.

And so he did. He split her head with an ax. But as he committed the act, her half sister unexpectedly entered the room. In a panic, he killed her too.

He had convinced himself that the extraordinary man wouldn't hesitate, wouldn't feel guilt, that carrying out the act would feel necessary, not criminal. That he would rise above morality.

I can't help but think of the recent murder everyone at the pub had been talking about. A young man, full of potential, shot the CEO of a major healthcare company in broad daylight—justice, he claimed, for corporate greed and his mother's untreated pain. He called it a symbolic act against parasitic power. Strangely, some people on social media praised him.

But my thoughts return to the Rebel, who is now speaking with increasing instability.

"I wore my philosophy like a cloak. But underneath it, I was trembling."

He recalls his faltering—his fear during the act, his panic when the half sister appeared. His escape had been frantic, not the calm, controlled act of someone who had transcended morality but the chaos of someone broken by it.

I shift in my seat, the weight of his words pressing uncomfortably in my chest. Another confession. Another horror story. The lecture feels stuck on repeat—each voice replaying the same philosophy in a different key, but every ending brutally alike.

The rest of his story traces the arc of psychological collapse. Though he wasn't caught, he couldn't escape the guilt. He sank into depression, forgot things, became delirious. He fainted after overhearing others discuss the murder. His mind unraveled. He struggled with the urge to confess. And yet, strangely, he kept returning to the scene of the crime, each visit deepening his despair.

In a moment of brief compassion, he showed kindness to

an alcoholic man down on his luck, someone whose misery reflected his own.

As he nears the end of his story, his failure becomes unmistakable. The extraordinary man he had idolized was a lie. His torment came not only from the murders but from the collapse of his entire belief system. The extraordinary man was supposed to rise above morality, but his guilt and fear exposed him as utterly ordinary. His philosophy had failed him. And he couldn't live with what he'd done—nor can he live with the fact that he couldn't live with it. He feels like a sinner.

The room falls silent again, heavy with the weight of his confession. It is no surprise when he refers to himself again as a louse.

From his story, I draw four truths:

1. In a world without God, morality becomes subjective.
2. In a world without God, people may idolize themselves and treat personal convictions as divine.
3. In a world without God, the conscience still convicts.
4. In a world without God, there is no true resolution for guilt, no hope for redemption.

THE PRINCIPLES FOR A HUMAN RELIGION

I don't know what I'd expected, but certainly not this. I hadn't come looking for the collapse of men, but that's what I've found. It's like watching the brakes fail—slow to start, then terrifying as the momentum grows. A philosophical car crash in motion. Four men, long dead, laid bare their lives before us. Not with remorse or wisdom but with the bizarre calm of those who've already paid the price and have nothing left to lose. No one moves. No one coughs. It isn't silence, it's suspension, the room hung from a thread.

What haunts me most isn't their suffering. It's their logic.

Each of them had followed the thread of self-will, of nihilism, of man-as-God and they hadn't turned back. They carried their ideas to their bitter end, and the result wasn't liberation. It was rot.

The words of 2 Timothy 3:1 cling to me: "There will be terrible times in the last days." It has always seemed exaggerated—lovers of self, proud and heartless. But now I see it: This is what happens when humanity worships itself. The chaos isn't accidental. It's the consequence. Meaning unmade, morality dismantled, every man a god until he destroys everything he touches.

Two suicides. One murderer. A man who watched his brother kill their father. And not one of them seems to have found the thing he was looking for. Each has tried to transcend the human condition, to rise above morality, conscience, or grief, and each has ended up devoured by it.

We do not bear the weight of godhood well. That much is clear. When we try, we don't become enlightened, we fracture. The very act of declaring ourselves divine seems to crack us open from the inside. They aren't indifferent, they are terrified. And now, so am I.

The moderator, astonishingly unfazed, wraps up the evening with a perfunctory smile. Another semester, another panel on the "principles for human religion." As if what we've just seen is another academic exercise, rather than the public autopsy of four souls.

A student next to me scoffs and says, "These lectures never end," stuffing his notebook into a bag. "All this talk and never a real answer." And he is right. Decades of ideas, centuries of thought, and nothing solid. Carl Sagan's old line returns, sterile and indifferent: "The cosmos is all that is or ever was or ever will be."[12]

But after tonight, that doesn't feel like enough. I have the suspicion that, beneath the silence, more than a few of us are secretly hoping for something more. Not reason or more science. But law. A voice. A command. Something unshakable.

But the modern mind cannot tolerate absolutes. That much is clear.

We file out, dazed. The air smells the same as it did when we came in, damp clothes, gum, and coffee. It makes me feel sick, but it clings. Phones light up in the darkness, thumbs already drafting tweets, looking up names. Everyone is trying to make sense of what we've just witnessed.

I pause beneath the stone archway at the entrance. Words carved overhead catch the light: "Human life has meaning because we create and develop our futures."[13]

I stare at it, bewildered. I know it is meant to inspire. But in the wake of those four lives, it strikes me as almost cruel. What if we can't create meaning? What if we were never meant to?

The lecture hall clicks shut behind me. I step into the street with the others, but something has shifted. The future doesn't feel like a promise anymore. It feels like a long, narrow corridor.

And Novemberton isn't just a town I'm walking through, it's the part of me that no longer knows where I'm going.

Chapter Six

STUCK IN SELF-DESTRUCT

I'd sell the whole world off for a farthing, straight off, so long as I was left in peace. Is the world to go to pot, or am I to go without my tea? I say that the world may go to pot for me as long as I always get my tea.

—The Underground Man, in Fyodor Dostoyevsky, *Notes from Underground*

I stand at the stone steps of the university library, and it feels like I've surfaced too fast from deep water; I hardly know where I am. The evening has dropped like a curtain, sudden and smothering. Streetlights crackle to life one by one, casting uneven circles of yellow light down the path. I glance toward the lawn, but it warps and bends, stretching out before me like a black pool of water. Faces blur into smears. Chatter turns to noise without shape. Dizziness tightens its grip. Sweat beads on my neck as my vision collapses the world into a narrowing corridor.

Nearby, a bench sits untouched by the whirl. I move toward it, making it only a few steps before I sit. My legs buckle under the weight of a dread I've carried all day.

A thousand things move around me, but my mind goes

backward. I'm in the abandoned town library again. Dust in my lungs, pages turning beneath my fingers. The fever of ideas—ancient, brilliant, failing. I see the words above the door I just walked through: "Human life has meaning because we create and develop our futures."

The smell of mint gum clings—sweet, synthetic, and sickening. Then the reel stutters—gunshot wound, rope-burned throat. The Hero. The Vanguard.

I feel betrayed. Has all this philosophy—systematized, dissected, and framed in logical architecture—ever truly understood the gravity of the human condition? Can fragile minds craft futures that don't collapse beneath the weight of their own flaws? What if philosophy is only as stable as the hands that write it? Then it is already broken.

And those four panelists, those walking testaments to nihilism, to self-will untethered, have made the best argument against their own godless religion. One verse from Scripture comes to me again. It fits the night too well: "Furthermore, just as they did not think it worthwhile to retain the knowledge of God, so God gave them over to a depraved mind, so that they do what ought not to be done" (Rom. 1:28).

This is what it looks like, I think. The rot that comes when the soul is handed over to itself. Not freedom but collapse. Hero, Vanguard, Thinker, Rebel, they each became the very proof of what they tried to deny. Each one thinking. Each one collapsing. Each one reasoning themselves into ruin.

And just when I think I can't take any more, I notice him. A hunched figure creeps along the edge of the courtyard. He mutters to himself, snickering like a kid who's hidden all the staplers in the university and can't wait for the fallout. He's disheveled, fidgety, and sunk in on himself like a collapsing tent. He slips into a side door just outside the streetlight. I follow. Of course I do. There's something about him, absurd and slightly terrifying, but I'm gripped.

Inside, the university feels different. Hollowed out. No conversations, just stillness and the smell of damp November air.

The halls stretch on forever, identical. I pass a drinking fountain, a trophy case, another fountain, and then I hear the muttering again, low and bitter. "I am a sick man. A spiteful man. My liver is diseased . . . No. I refuse to consult a doctor—out of spite."[1]

I follow the voice to a door marked "IT." Through a crack, I see him slumped at a desk, muttering to a monitor in a space so small it could be mistaken for a janitor's closet. It's claustrophobic, half lit, dust laced. A messy office, if you can call it that, crammed with old computers, cables, and junk. He types furiously, his words a strange mix of tech jargon and self-hatred. As I watch, he writes an email but doesn't send it. Instead, he flicks to a folder—*Drafts*. I see dozens of unsent messages, and I can't tell whether he's too afraid to send them or just thinks it's beneath him.

I knock. He startles, then grins. Whether from glee or menace, I can't tell. He waves me in like an old friend, then immediately regrets it, sighing like he's just committed a crime. He doesn't ask for my name. Doesn't give his. Just launches into a tirade about the lecture as if we'd been discussing it all evening. I never saw him in the room, but somehow he knows every word. "Heard it from the hall," he mutters. "They probably saved me a seat, but I couldn't be bothered."

The Hero, the Vanguard, the Thinker, and the Rebel are all problematic to the IT guy. He mocks their grand declarations, their philosophies, and their reliance on reason. Driven by inner turmoil, he protests that these are pathetic attempts to control the chaos of human existence. It's all a form of self-serving rationalization, he claims, and the four panelists should know better than to think that science or philosophy can provide answers to life's meaninglessness.

Amid the clutter of the IT guy's piles of junk, my eyes catch an old piano keyboard. One key stands out—dirtied and worn—a clear sign that it's been pressed more often than the others. He notices me staring, and his irritation is palpable. My eyes wander for just a moment, and that alone seems to bother him. Abruptly, he shifts his monologue, his focus turning to the keyboard. He picks it up with one hand and places it on his lap. Then, with almost mechanical detachment, he taps the key over and over, its repetitive sound growing more grating with each press. His gaze never leaves mine as he laughs lightly, amused by the moment.

"For the whole work of man really seems to consist in nothing but proving to himself every minute that he is a man, and not a piano key!" His words, sharp and pointed, match the rhythm of the tapping key. "It may cost him his skin; it may lead to cannibalism! Even if man *were* nothing but a piano key . . . he'd still do something perverse, out of sheer ingratitude, just to make his point."[2]

Despite his deranged, eccentric nature, I notice a clarity to his thinking. If science is all that defines human existence, then people are reduced to nothing more than piano keys: predictable, mechanical responses to external stimuli. That's why he believes the panelists failed—they tried to understand their existence through logic and reason when they should have known better. To him, life is chaos, not orderly science and philosophy.

Rational systems, irrational people.

The four panelists were caught in the trap of intellect, snared by the very rationale they tried to wield. They didn't realize it, but they were struggling to escape from being nothing more than piano keys.

His hand continues to tap the key, each press deliberate, mocking. His smirk deepens, he relishes the fact that he knows more than me. He believes he's superior—smarter, more intellectually aware—simply because he's conscious of the complexity of the human condition. He thinks the panelists missed this crucial understanding. None of them were willing to embrace the chaos and irrationality of life.

It clicks. I suddenly understand why he hides in his broom-closet office, why no one knows him on campus, why he revels in the anonymity of being the IT guy. Why he creeps around at night, listening to lectures from the hallway. Why he refuses medical attention, even as his liver aches. Why he writes cruel emails but never sends them. It's all part of his pursuit of freedom and individuality, a way to prove, to both himself and the world, that he's not bound by anyone's expectations: not social, scientific, philosophical, rational, or moral. He embraces his irrationality as a final act of resistance, a rebellion against the same trap that ensnared the panelists, even as they thought they were breaking free.

THE IT GUY AND THE SECURITY GUARD

The IT guy drifts into an old memory and begins unraveling a story—another night slinking around the university campus. But this time, a fight broke out at a bar, and one of the brawlers was thrown through a window. He envied that man. So he charged into the bar, hoping to pick a fight and get tossed through a window too.

As he stood there, eager for confrontation, he accidentally blocked a walkway. A police officer grabbed him by the shoulders and shoved him aside.

> I had been treated like a fly.[3]

He considered provoking the officer just to be thrown through the window. But he didn't. He insists it wasn't cowardice. He works overtime to convince me he had the guts to fight, to be beaten, to go crashing through glass.

Suddenly, he flips his tone. With an air of superiority, he expounds on why no one in the bar was worth his time—or his intellect. Arguing with the officer, he insists, would have confounded the imbeciles in the bar, leaving them bewildered by his eloquence.

Resentment festered. He brooded over the incident for years. He went so far as to follow the officer around campus, studying his every move.

> I stared at him with spite and hatred, and so it went on . . . for several years. My resentment grew even deeper with years.

Even in my wildest dreams, I've never encountered such pettiness.

His obsession escalated. He scoured the university database for records, pay stubs—anything to uncover the officer's name and home address. At times, he trailed him back to his residence.

Then he hatched a plan for revenge: He would write a defamatory article, altering the officer's name just enough to make him recognizable. He submitted it anonymously to *The Novemberton Grey*, the university newspaper, but they never published it.

His resentment deepened.

He drafted a letter challenging the officer to a fight, convinced it would intimidate him into an apology and a friendship. He even entertained the thought of their camaraderie.

> He could have shielded me with his higher rank, while I could have improved his mind.[4]

He cringes at the memory of that letter, relieved he never sent it.

A more elaborate scheme took shape while he walked along the Dreadwater, the river that borders the university.

> I used to stroll along the Dreadwater, though it was hardly a stroll so much as a series of innumerable miseries, humiliations, and resentments. I used to wriggle along like an eel, continually moving aside for professors, women, and deans. I was a minnow that was continually making way for everyone.[5]

Oddly, he relished that feeling.

Then he noticed something. The officer often walked the same path, stepping aside for professors, deans, and women—but never for him. The officer walked forward, unfazed, leaving the IT guy to move aside every time.

He began waking in the night, asking himself, "Why must you always be the first to move aside?" He devised a plan to collide with the officer. He obsessed over it, even considering what he would wear. The thought consumed him so much that he took out two loans—one as an advance from the university, the other from his supervisor—to purchase an expensive suit for the occasion.

He wore the suit on his strolls along the river, rehearsing the moment again and again. Yet when the moment arrived, he faltered. Time after time, he stepped aside. Then one day he clenched his eyes shut and rammed shoulder to shoulder into the officer.

> He did not even look around! He pretended not to notice, but he was only pretending. I am convinced of that!

I get the impression he's projecting, lost in self-delusion.

> I returned home feeling that I was fully avenged for everything . . . I sang like Pavarotti![6]

But as time passed, reality settled in. The officer had not noticed him at all. Years of plotting had led to an anticlimactic moment that left him humiliated, feeling the weight of his own insignificance.

> I felt very sick afterward.

THE IT GUY AND HIS FRAT BROTHERS

The office feels like it's shrinking around me, tightening under the pressure of his erratic energy and wild ideas. Without warning, the IT guy launches into the next story—one about his fraternity brothers. Years ago, they were all part of the same frat at the University of Novemberton, though he never truly fit in. One day, he ran into a few of his old friends.

> They looked upon me as something on the level of a common fly.

The guys were planning a dinner at the finest steakhouse in town, The Black Oak. It was a big send-off for their old frat brother Victor. He had recently taken a high-profile job in a large city. Everybody liked Victor. But the IT guy hated him. He hated his self-confidence, his handsome face, his success—everything, right down to the tone of his voice.

Yet the IT guy invited himself to the dinner.

> It seemed to me that to invite myself would be unexpected and that they would all be conquered at once . . . that they would look at me with respect.[7]

Knowing that he and Victor had never gotten along, the frat brothers seemed uncomfortable with his presence. Still, they told him to show up at The Black Oak at 5:00 p.m. the next night, making it clear it was a private event and that he wasn't exactly welcome.

"This isn't a free meal!" one of them reminded him as he walked away. He still owed them money and had no idea how he'd pay.

The IT guy hated these guys, and they hated him; he wonders what on earth had possessed him to want to attend. He trails off, mumbling about his hatred for their endless conversations about football and women, spiraling into complaints about their crude tastes and pathetic intellect. He speaks of how he read academic journals just to know things they never would—to prove he was smarter.

The mumbling sharpens. His haughtiness returns.

> I did not desire their affection; on the contrary, I continually longed for their humiliation.[8]

He reasoned that he would not pay his credit card bill that month just to have the money to attend.

The next night, he left work early to get ready. As he put on his suit, he noticed it was now old, stained in a few places, and didn't fit quite right. He wouldn't look dignified, but that didn't stop him any more than being broke did.

> I dreamed of getting the upper hand . . . making them like me, if only for my elevation of thought. I dreamed that I should crush Victor.

Then, as usual, he vacillates, insisting he didn't really care what happened. I can't help but wonder what kind of self-delusion still fills his head as he tells the story.

As he tells me about calculating his perfect entrance, determining the precise moment to arrive for maximum impact, the IT guy scribbles something on a Post-it: "Power is timing." Then he immediately balls it up and tosses it into the trash. The note lands somewhere among others, I assume.

But when he pushed open the doors to The Black Oak, no one was there. He wasn't just first, he was alone. The waitstaff looked up, mildly confused; the restaurant had barely opened. He was forced to sit in silence and watch them lay out the silverware. A server offered him water—I think it was kind; he sees it as pathetic. He didn't want water. It was free.

An hour later, his friends finally arrived and greeted him with generic courtesy and indifference, making him feel insignificant and out of place. He bickered with them about being late, which only added to the awkwardness.

The conversation soon turned to his job, which embarrassed him. He was still at the university, working a low-paying job in IT and data processing. One of the guys scoffed, "How can an IT guy afford to eat at The Black Oak?" To which he made an off-putting comment about earning a living while the others there lived off of privilege.

Victor, sensing the rising tension, changed the topic, diving into stories about his latest love triangles and sports betting. The group laughed while the IT guy burned with embarrassment and insecurity.

> The brutes acted like it was an honor for me to sit with them. It was an honor to them and not to me!

He sat in fury, the stain on his clothes seeming to grow larger with every minute. His embarrassment only made him more determined to insult them.

While Victor told a story about one of his wealthy friends, the IT guy slipped in an insult, asking why that friend wasn't with them at the steak house that night.

> Victor, without a word, examined me as though I were an appalling insect.[9]

Finally, it came time to toast Victor. Everyone raised their glasses with their best wishes. The IT guy stood up without warning, nearly knocking over his chair. He lifted his glass with absurd glee.

> To the fraternity . . . and the unbreakable bond of brotherhood . . . or at least, the illusion of it.

He chuckles while telling me this, savoring every word—fidgeting with his fingers, just like when I first saw him in the university yard.

The frat brothers called him a miserable loser and candidly told him it was a mistake letting him come. Their conversation continued, and they acted as though he didn't exist. He remained in his chair, conflicted, with cold sweat collecting on his forehead. He refused to leave. Occasionally, he'd take gulps of his coffee, just for attention.

The brothers finally left in a cab to head to a pub—without the IT guy. He crept through the town, hating his frat brothers all the more, but even more so himself.

I walked as though spat upon.

THE IT GUY AND THE ONE-NIGHT STAND

Before I have any chance of excusing myself, or finding a way out of this room, the IT guy grabs my head and awkwardly shoves it toward the wall behind his desk. It's completely bare—except for a single twenty-dollar bill taped dead center. Wrinkled. Yellowing slightly at the corners. It's clearly been there for some time.

He suddenly plummets into the rest of his torrid tale. That same night, humiliated and half delirious, he wandered into a bar—and met *her.* She was a young woman with a pale face, a good-natured smile, and a tragic air she couldn't quite mask. They struck up an awkward conversation, and somehow it ended with his following her back to her apartment. As they walked inside, he caught a glimpse of himself in the reflection of her building's glass door. He looked repulsive—no, revolting.

"I was glad for it; glad I could seem repulsive to her," he says.[10]

The following morning, he woke up next to her, swallowed by misery, and noticed her staring at him with cold, detached eyes. The look unsettled him. They started talking, and through their exchange, he learned her name and about her past. It was a sad life full of sorrow and regret.

This led him into a long diatribe—mostly made up—about life, love, and *cheap love*, and how their night together was hideous. To his surprise, she agreed. The thought that she might have been thinking the same thing as she stared at him bothered him deeply. He felt a need to regain his superiority.

"It was the fact that I could exercise my power over her that attracted me the most," he admits.

To assert this power and reclaim his intellectual dominance, he unleashed a monologue of condemnation. He told her how women who seek hookups in bars are doomed to be discarded by society. How men would use her, then forget her. That in a year, she would be worthless.

After his pontifications, she retorted with a single word: "Bookish."[11]

It crushed him.

He wanted to be Nietzsche. She saw him as a librarian.

In anger, he doubled down on what he was saying, cruelty flowing from his lips.

> No one will bless you, no one will sigh for you, they will only want to get rid of you as soon as possible . . . they won't even waste time fighting over you.[12]

I've come to understand the IT guy is erratic and intense, but this shocks me—the lengths he went to manipulate her, asserting his superiority to quell his insecurity.

Naturally, it broke her spirit.

Conflicted, he suggested she come by his university office sometime. Before leaving, she pulled out a letter from her desk. It was from a student at the university who genuinely cared for her, an admirer unaware of who she really was.

> The poor girl was keeping that student's letter as a precious treasure, and had to run to fetch it, her only treasure, because she didn't want me to leave without knowing that she, too, was honestly and genuinely loved . . . No doubt that letter was destined to sit in her desk and lead to nothing.[13]

And yet the letter bothered him. He's visibly shaken by the memory.

All of a sudden his anger and cruelty make sense. It hits me as my gaze moves from the twenty-dollar bill to the strange, hunched man hidden in his broom closet: He knows he has no treasures to prove *he* is lovable.

On his way home, he began to fear that she would visit him. He worried that if she did, she would see he was only an IT guy, not a professor, and all of his intellectual superiority would crumble. He would fail as her savior.

He worried for days, wishing he'd said something cruel enough to keep her away. In his mind, she was someone he could refine and develop. She would eventually fall at his feet, loving him completely, while he remained indifferent. Never reciprocating.

One day, she showed up. A quick glance around the room was all it took for her to see the fast-food wrappers, scattered papers, and pathetic mess.

He was crushed. The jig was up.

He insisted he wasn't ashamed of his office or his position as the IT guy. I could tell he was deluding himself again.

Then, in a flurry, he rushed across the hall to fetch his intern and begged him to go to the coffee shop to get them tea. When he returned, he began ranting to her about his intern, how much he hated him and how the intern made his life miserable. It was a way to manipulate her, to make her believe he was the victim of his circumstances. His anger at himself intensified. He took it out on her.

He told her he hated her. To his surprise, she understood him more than he realized. He was so used to being "bookish" he didn't know how to process their encounter. Despite this, she showed genuine care for him by embracing him. But the more she embraced him, the more conflicted he became—drawn to her yet repulsed by her.

He admitted to her, "I am a scoundrel, a sluggard, and a

villain . . . the nastiest, stupidest, absurdist, and most envious of all the worms of the earth."[14]

He fessed up to playing games with her, and I realize it was self-punishment, an attempt to earn her pity. But she embraced him all the more, and it humiliated him further.

He doesn't understand it. He tells me, "I cannot get on without domineering and tyrannizing over someone, but . . . there is no explaining anything by reason, and so it is useless to reason."[15]

His hatred grew deeper the more she embraced him. Finally, she grasped that he was incapable of loving her. He didn't want affection, he wanted peace. To be left alone in his IT office.

> Real life oppressed me so much I could hardly breathe.

Then he did the unthinkable while driving her away: He gave her money. The money was to pay for the drink she'd had when they met. It was a reminder that she—and all this—was nothing more than a hookup. A pointless one-night stand.

She left the money behind. And he never saw her again. All he was left with was the painful weight of his soul, memorialized on his bare wall.

He reflects: "This cruelty came from my evil brain . . . made up so completely, a product of the brain and of books."

I gather that, on one hand, books had constructed his life. But on the other, they contributed to his demise: They failed to capture the raw, messy nature of human existence.

He concludes, "We are oppressed at being men—men with a real individual body and blood; we are ashamed of it; we think it a disgrace and try to contrive to be some sort of impossible generalized man."[16]

As his fingers tap the keyboard, I find myself back on the park bench. The lawn stretches out, crisp and clean. Lucidity returns to my mind. Shapeless conversations untangle into words. The streetlights blink back to life, casting their soft glow down the path again.

As soon as my legs steady, I run to see the IT guy, needing to say some kind of goodbye. But the side door he entered is now blocked by iron scaffolding. It's under repair, though it looks like no one has touched it in ages.

I glance back at the park bench, unsure, curious, confused. In spite of his urging to forget him, I suspect I'll remember him most of all.

My brief encounter with him has left four unforgettable thoughts, each of which he would inevitably find a way to complicate.

1. *Humans are messy.* Humans often act irrationally, and no matter how rational they are, humans can't always fix themselves.
2. *Human freedom is overwhelming.* Without divine law or purpose, making choices that lead to peace and fulfillment can be torturous and end in self-sabotage and more suffering.
3. *More thinking isn't always the answer.* Human struggles aren't always solved by what's in a book; they're deep, emotional, mysterious, and unpredictable.
4. *Without something bigger, humans are at risk of decay.* Without a connection to something that transcends the self, humans often end up isolated, lost, and stuck in self-destruction.

DOSTOYEVSKY'S WARNING

As I look up from the park bench toward the university again, my mind drifts to Fyodor Dostoyevsky, the nineteenth-century Russian novelist. Odd—I don't remember seeing his books in the library. Of all the books I pulled from the shelves, the stories I devoured, his were absent. But now, suddenly, they seem alive in my mind. If any novels speak of Novemberton, his do.

Dostoyevsky's novels unfold in the everyday landscape of Russia during a time of political nihilism when revolutionaries, driven by intellect, discarded traditional morality and religious conventions. While Nietzsche wasn't widely read in Russia at the time, these intellectuals were, in a way, willing to power by dismantling their moral structures to create new ones that served their personal needs. This intellectual revolution was led by the German and French elite. The younger generation of Russians embraced it, pushing these ideas to extremes, attempting to tear down the old order in the name of progress. Russian Orthodoxy, long the pillar of Russian society, was on the chopping block.[17]

Dostoyevsky rejected this movement with all fierceness.

In an age of meaninglessness, when science declared the death of God, Nietzsche saw an opportunity for humans to transcend old morality and forge new values. Dostoyevsky, however, believed the opposite. He saw a return to faith, humility, and love as the answer. Without a religious foundation, society would decay.

Dostoyevsky's novels are a warning. His characters—some of the most authentic in literature—are cold, intellectual, mechanical. (Consider how they embody the Hero, the Vanguard, the Thinker, the Rebel, and, yes, the IT guy.) But they all end in despair and moral crisis. Their intellect, books, and rational frameworks can't account for the complexity of human suffering, spiritual needs, and dilemmas. Dostoyevsky's characters demonstrate that a world without God, when lived out in everyday reality rather than philosophical theory, leads both individuals and societies to decay in the cold November of their souls.

Dostoyevsky's novels challenge an intellectual society adrift in meaninglessness with the riddle of the self. When you encounter his characters, you often encounter yourself. They are our doubles, each bearing a secret wound: the search for meaning. These characters emerge from the most ordinary settings, from gray existences like our own, much like Novemberton, struggling to redeem their inner void—in dark alleys, bars, brothels, and damp apartments. Without God, they rely on intellect and higher reasoning for purpose, but this leads only to self-exaltation and self-destruction. By the end of his novels, there are no towering German or French philosophers. Only prisons, asylums, and suicide remain. Dostoyevsky's message is clear: The problem of meaninglessness can be solved only in the God whom modern humanity has buried and forgotten.

Something in me beckons me to move forward, to leave the hollow halls of the university behind. The gleaming fortress of intellect, and all its grandeur, contrasts with the sight of the city behind it, languishing in decay.

Then from the inky blackness a streak of blood-red light emerges, pulsing, and with it the noise surges forth.

— Chapter Seven —

THE PLAGUE SETTLES IN

But what does it mean, the plague? It's life, that's all.

—Albert Camus, *The Plague*

The scream of an ambulance shatters the stillness of the night, taking my pulse with it. Sirens stacking on sirens, like the city decided to cry all at once.

I know immediately: something is wrong.

I take off toward the center of town, heart hammering. Streets that once pulsed with noise now feel strangely thin, the sirens trailing behind them a stillness that lets the fear in me grow.

I reach Rational Care Medical and everything blurs at once—lights, motion, shouting. Emergency lights flash, pooling against the walls like blood. There are people everywhere, bystanders shouting over one another, reporters pushing in with cameras half raised, and police frantically trying to push the crowd back. A woman stands crying. Someone else is filming her.

I push through, half walking, half carried with the current—and then I see him.

A child. No more than five.

He's taken from the ambulance, half shielded by the distress around him. His eyes, wide beneath an oversized oxygen mask, are too still for a child's face. Fragile, he clutches his teddy bear, so tightly that his knuckles are white.

A paramedic, in the kind of suit I've seen only in movies, waves frantically to clear the doors. And for a second, the noise rises so sharply it becomes static. Then drops out entirely. Just flashing lights, the stretcher vanishing into glass, and the terrible sound of nothing.

People begin to whisper. Spreading like wildfire, theories are born and mutated midsentence. But it doesn't matter what they are saying. I know what they are trying to outrun.

The murmuring dies down, but its ghost lingers—stifled sobs, sentences trailing off before they're done.

He said he wasn't feeling well, but they thought it was just a cold.

He's strong; kids bounce back.

He was smiling yesterday.

We stand outside the hospital under the black sky. Fluorescent light spills from the windows. A few people lean against the brick, but most just stand still. No one looks at each other when they speak. Nobody prays, but nobody leaves.

The collective realization has settled in—that a child's suffering is the one thing that cannot be ignored, the one horror that demands explanation, and the one silence that should never be left unbroken.[1]

I picture him just yesterday, running laps at recess, trading fruit snacks, bragging that his mom and dad were taking him to the zoo to see the otters. And now? Now he has a name no one has heard of before—neural fog plague.

They say it came from the lake. Some rare bacterial strain caught in the dense November air—a slow-moving fog, invisible and fatal. Causing neurological disintegration.

And then we find out he has died.

The administrator makes a statement I can barely take in. Something about systems. Procedures. Testing protocols. It feels like they are speaking through gauze.

The boy has died.

Novemberton has always carried a quiet dread. But this—this is different.

There have been as many plagues as wars in history. But people never think *they're* next. And when death came, it came first for a child. Not a criminal. Not a revolutionary. A child.[2]

And in an instant, we are all the same—equal in a way no one wants. Equal in exposure.

Equal in fear.[3]

THE INDIFFERENT UNIVERSE

The death of a child has a way of undoing everything.

Not just the emotions, rage, panic, grief but the framework. The scaffolding we use to make sense of the world.

In the stillness outside the hospital, it becomes clear: All the systems we've built—reason, science, belief, progress—they are too small. Too clean. They've worked until this. Until a five-year-old vanishes behind glass and no one can explain why.

The questions don't come loudly. They itch, quietly, beneath the skin. The kind that keep you awake at night, staring at the ceiling, asking not just what happened but what does this mean? And worse, does it mean anything at all?

Whatever answers this town thinks it has, none of them can hold this.

That's when I remember Albert Camus. I'd been reading him in the library. Something about his stubborn refusal to look away from the raw edge of things comforts me. He doesn't try to rescue meaning from chaos. He just sees it, that dry, clear-eyed stare at the world.

That's what makes him believable. He never tries to explain suffering. He refuses to dress it in theology or tuck it into a system—he hated systems. Instead, he looks at it. In stories, essays, and plays. He wrote philosophy that bled.

And standing there outside the hospital, the same mechanical, unrelenting beeping still in my ears, I remember another room. A hallway. Beige walls. That brittle fluorescent light that only hospitals know how to cast.

I remember my mother. Tubes and wires weaving a web that felt both vital and cruel. How small her hand felt in mine. How big the world felt around us.

There were no answers then either. Only breath. Only waiting. Only that dull ache behind the eyes that never quite became tears.

And now, here it is again. The same weight. But this time, the child isn't me.

Camus would have understood that. Not the facts of it but the feeling. The scale of it. The lack of explanation. He didn't try to name the grief. He just stood in it. And wrote.

Camus had seen it firsthand. Raised in religion, broken by war. Shaped by poverty and a deaf mother who taught him silence. He lost his father to one world war and then endured another. And through it all, he noticed something most people work hard to unsee: The universe isn't handing out answers. It isn't cruel or kind. It simply *is*, utterly indifferent.

You could say he believed in a closed system. That nothing existed outside the physical universe—no higher mind, no divine ledger, no comforting arc bending toward justice. Just molecules, weather, gravity, chance. And so when a child dies for no reason, when a town waits outside a hospital with nothing but their breath and their hands in their pockets, that, to Camus, is the real world.

That's the absurd.

We long for meaning, and the world just keeps turning. We tell stories, and the sky doesn't flinch. If anything makes sense, it's only because we're good at patterns. Like staring at toast and thinking you see Elvis. But the toaster doesn't care. Burn marks don't mean anything. You just make them mean something.

Camus said the absurd wasn't just about suffering. It was the mismatch between the human heart and the mute mechanics of the universe.

It isn't just that the child has died. It's that nothing stopped it. Nothing noticed. Nothing cared.

And that's when it hits me. In a place like this, there wouldn't be a sign. No voice in the sky. No thread tying this to some higher plan.

Just this silence.

And still—I stay.

I watch.

And I whisper to myself, "So be it."

But I will not look away.

INFOBESITY AND THE ABSURD

I know, almost immediately, that this is just the beginning for Novemberton.

The boy's name, the phrase *neural fog plague*, the blood-red lights outside the hospital—none of it will stay sacred for long. It will trend. It will be memed and it will circulate.

It will move through podcasts, threads, comment sections, timelines. I can already see it—screens lit up in every window, faces turned down, everyone feeding on it. Sure, people will say they are unsettled by the death toll, the emergency mandates, and the innocent suffering, but that won't be the most disturbing part. The real horror will be quieter. It will be the reminder, day after day, post after post, of just how absurd life really is. How random and fragile. How utterly out of place we are in an indifferent, unfeeling universe.

Thomas Nagel, in his philosophical wisdom, says something that hints at the cost of infobesity: "Reflection on our minuteness and brevity appears to be intimately connected with the sense that life is meaningless."[4]

The more information we get, the more minute, and thus absurd, we feel. This is because absurdism is perceiving our true situation. The more we know, the less it makes sense.

Remember the zettabytes? Exactly.

Not only is the information highway expanding, it is speeding us straight into existential nausea. The great equation of the digital age: the sum of all scrolling. Add it all up—the beauty plus the tragedy, the love plus the hate, the wins plus the losses—and what do you get?

A giant, cosmic zero-sum game, it would seem.

Because the more people scroll, the more the universe rubs it in. Dash-cam wrecks. Predator-prey footage. Apocalyptic weather shredding cities. Toss in the latest update on rogue black holes and doomsday asteroids, and suddenly Mom and Dad's fiftieth anniversary feels flimsy. Great. Mike and Lisa are having a boy—cool. But what if he catches the plague? Or worse, what if a Komodo dragon crashes his birthday party one day and eats everyone? What then? (That kind of stuff has happened, ya know.)

Information has a way of whispering an ugly truth: There are winners and losers, but in the end, everybody loses.

And that is fundamentally incompatible with the human need for meaning, for permanence, for some grand cosmic reassurance that it all adds up to something.

But what if it doesn't? As the plague spreads through Novemberton, another sickness takes hold. A second plague, equally insidious.

The plague of absurdity. It's more than just the cold November of the soul. It's the gut-wrenching realization that the universe doesn't give a damn. And if you doubt it, just wait until the next riptide drags a father of three out to sea. See how much the universe cares then.

CONFRONTING THE ABSURD

The days that followed blurred together. The boy was gone, yet the fog remained. I walked the streets of Novemberton like someone trying to remember something they'd never really known. This place was getting to me, the grief and disorientation. The absurdity of it all curling around doorways and lingering in the streets.

People responded how they always do when the universe speaks in silence. Some acted, some laughed, others resumed business. Maybe it didn't matter. What if it was never really about the plague, but what the plague revealed?

I started watching people, not out of judgment but in awe. How they scrambled to build meaning from the wreckage, each one clinging to a different thread.

The Activist

The first figure to stand out in Novemberton was a community activist who took swift action. She was convinced the crisis could have been prevented if health officials had paid closer attention to the town's water system. She demanded an investigation, certain the city would resist, knowing the exposure would reveal years of agricultural runoff, pesticide buildup, and politicians quietly tied to chemical companies.

Each day, she stood at the city center holding a sign: "FOG PLAGUE KILLS—ACTION NOW!" What started with a handful of supporters quickly grew into a formidable movement. But as the numbers swelled, so did the opposition. Within days, counterprotesters appeared, accusing the activists of spreading conspiracy theories and stoking panic. The activists fired back, claiming their opponents were protecting corporate greed, special interests, and societal privilege.

I overheard her tell a reporter, "People say it isn't real, that it's a bad dream that will pass. But in this bad dream, a child died because the city failed its people."

She refused to relent. News reports claimed she was

forming an independent task force. She urged cities beyond Novemberton to scrutinize their water systems and condemned the federal emergency management agency for dragging its feet on relief stations.

With each action, backlash intensified. Rage matched her resolve. Dialogue disintegrated.

Both sides radicalized and the violence that erupted in the streets began to spread like a second plague.

The Columnist

As the crisis deepened, a once-unknown columnist rose to prominence in Novemberton. His sharp insights struck a nerve, earning him sudden attention. Until now, his career had wandered in obscurity, but the plague forced the town into self-reflection, and his words gave shape to an unease long kept quiet.

Unlike others, he brought religion back into public discussion, not as dogma but as a necessary structure for survival. He made no claims of certainty. He offered no proof. Instead, he argued that the soul cannot bear what the mind demands it accept: that the universe is closed, cold, and meaningless.

His influence grew. Every talk show, every social channel—his commentary filled them all, pushing religion back onto the table as an essential tool for human survival.

He became a polarizing figure. For some, his words brought hope. For others, they reeked of regression, a dangerous retreat from modern thought. But the backlash was swift, especially when he began speaking not just as a philosopher but as someone who had actually suffered. He didn't argue from abstraction. He reasoned from the ground, where the grief was real and the questions couldn't be ignored.

My sense of him has shifted over my time here. At first, he seemed like another public intellectual, piecing together conclusions from psychology, history, and faith. But during the plague, it became clear: He was bridging the gap to the transcendent and working something out with hope, not certainty. And that gave his words a different weight.

The Celebrity

The celebrity's presence in Novemberton during the plague stirred no less controversy than the others. She happened to be in town filming a movie when the neural fog plague struck. As panic spread, she turned to social media and, at least in the town's eyes, exploited the crisis to expand her audience. Several times a day, she posted about her online shopping habits. Fearing the plague, she stayed indoors while box after box arrived at her doorstep for unboxing and reviews: cosmetics, handbags, kitchen gadgets, and bedding, "because you deserve the best sleep when you're at home during the plague!"

While the cold universe watched innocents die, she took action by launching her own activewear line. Mostly yoga leggings in cleansing neutrals, with limited-edition pastels. Why not? Her daily livestreamed yoga sessions had grown a loyal following, more than capable of driving sales.

These sessions were far from dull. Often, while stretching, she'd mix in gossip with relationship advice that often read like lines from a vampire romance. "If your relationship is scandalous, step back and ask, Is this love, or is this infatuation—and addiction? Passion is exciting, and you deserve passion, but you also need security."

As the plague ravaged Novemberton, claiming more victims, the celebrity and her followers were focused on their own needs. In an online interview with an influencer outside the city, she defended her choices, claiming her approach wasn't insensitive but therapeutic.

One critic was less than generous: "In short, the plague suits her. It's an accomplice, a delightful accomplice." And maybe it was. The plague created the perfect conditions for her to thrive, fulfill her ambitions, and indulge in her pleasures: shopping, fitness, gossip, and expanding her influence. If she proved anything, it was that for some, individualism was the perfect cure for the plague.

The Delivery Driver

Also in Novemberton during the plague is a delivery driver cruising the streets in a red 2010 Ford Fiesta. On his bumper, a sticker that elicited smirks, said, "Still here. Still confused. Still driving." Unmoved by the town's panic, he delivered hamburgers, oversized burritos, and buffalo wings with ranch to residents huddling in fear of the next victim.

His reputation rested on his strangely passionate, oddly detached approach to feeding the town. As awkward as his car, he was known for his poorly timed conversations at the door. It wasn't unusual for him to say things like, "Enjoy the dumplings, they could be your last." Some customers requested another driver to avoid another tangent on how aliens built the pyramids. Clearly a podcast junkie—his oversized headphones never left his ears—he likely unwound with Reddit after work.

He seemed to have checked out of the usual narratives. Indifferent to the commentary on the plague, he kept delivering food without engaging in the drama. His strangeness was, at times, admirable: He still found a way to appreciate life's smaller pleasures. But his detachment often rubbed people the wrong way, and felt less like peace and more like apathy. Still, he didn't seem to care. He'd given up on finding meaning or justice—on mourning the innocent child, blaming the city, or tracing the arc of empire through tragedy. That was for someone else to sort out. He just brought the fries.

Once, a customer told him to be careful out there. His usual response, delivered flatly: "Thanks. I don't want to die, but if I do, then oh well. Now, enjoy your grub."

DEALING WITH THE PLAGUE

The figures who stay with me the most in Novemberton come from different places, but they have one thing in common: None of them remained indifferent to the indifference. And true indifference is impossible, as Camus understood well. Even choosing not to care is still a kind of response. You can't really opt out. Not when the world refuses to look away.

Each of them responded in their own way:

- The activist responded to the indifference through action: She acted her way toward meaning.
- The columnist responded to the indifference through thought: He reasoned his way toward meaning.
- The celebrity responded to the indifference through opportunism: She indulged her way toward meaning.
- The delivery driver responded to the indifference through irony: He humored his way toward meaning.

Acting. Thinking. Indulging. Humoring.

Four ways of navigating a universe that doesn't care. Four ways of coping with the silence.

None of them reintegrate God—not truly.

In a modern world, a closed system, as Camus called it, God can't be summoned just because the darkness deepens. You can't drag him back in just because the suffering becomes unbearable. That would undo everything modernity worked to dismantle. It would mean pretending we forgot what we learned.

Camus had no patience for that kind of forgetting. If a Christian influencer showed up during the plague with a ring light and a revival hashtag—"Pray for Novemberton!"—Camus wouldn't argue. He'd dismiss it outright. A coping mechanism and false solution, nothing more.

To that, he once wrote that

> to give these soothing potions the slightest efficacy, we would have to behave as if we had forgotten all our knowledge . . . pretend, in fact, to wipe out what is indelible. With one stroke of the pen [or one viral TikTok] we should have to cross out the contributions of several centuries . . .

> In short, we were worth nothing during the Renaissance, the eighteenth century, and the Revolution. We counted for something only from the tenth to the thirteenth century . . . All this has been in vain. And it is we who are nihilists![5]

It's a brutal paragraph. And it leaves little room for sentiment.

If that doesn't land, here's the blunt version: Camus thought the real nihilist wasn't the atheist, it was the Christian influencer with the broccoli haircut, dressed like it's 1995, giving the "go God" speeches. That's not revelation, nor is it revival. It's will to power dressed up as faith. A preferred reality, imposed under divine branding.

Nietzsche at least had the decency to leave God buried. Camus took that seriously. He remembered the madman. The lantern. The blood. Dragging God back into this mess now, after the death of the child, after the silence of the universe, isn't comfort. It's a rejection of everything we're supposed to have faced. It's philosophical suicide, dressed in Sunday clothes.

The world moved on. It left the gods behind. And now, trying to bring them back, not with reverence but with reels, isn't courage. It's retreat.

A society that claims to function in a closed system has to live like it does. Even when the fog comes. Especially then.

But that gets messy.

MEANING IN A CLOSED SYSTEM

A godless world sounds nice in theory. But as Camus warned, a plague always shows up.

A plague can drive people to despise God and long for a world without him. Yet it can also provoke the opposite question: Can anyone truly accept a world where the suffering of a child holds no meaning at all?

What happens when the principles of a human religion,

along with the rituals and stories we use to make sense of what doesn't last, are left solely in the hands of an activist, a columnist, a celebrity, and a delivery driver? What does that world look like?

As the neural fog plague spreads, I keep replaying the panel discussion, not out of curiosity but out of something closer to dread.

The voices I tried to forget now echo with a kind of terrible clarity. I can still see them—smiling, polished, flippant.

They spoke like the world was stable. Like truth was theirs to reshape. Like a child's suffering was an unfortunate footnote in the story of progress. And now their words ring louder than they should. There's something almost literary about them. Uncanny, even. Like they've stepped straight out of Dostoyevsky, out of his darkest warnings, and taken a seat on stage. They are not caricatures. They are products of modernity. Children of a rebellion that launched what some called "the great offensive against a hostile heaven."[6] Thinkers like Feuerbach, Marx, Nietzsche, Chernyshevsky—voices of defiance who promised freedom in a world without God. But something went wrong. Not a glitch, a catastrophe. Instead of bringing liberation, their philosophies helped grease the wheels for gulags, concentration camps, and killing fields. The war against God backfired, badly. In trying to escape divine tyranny, humankind ended up justifying the very horrors they once blamed on the divine.

As Camus put it, every rebellion against God has led to "crashing ramparts."[7]

Without God, we were free, but only to become gods ourselves. Man-gods, wielding the same prerogatives as the deity we claimed to hate. But the way we dealt with meaninglessness, modernity's prized inheritance, looked less like freedom and more like license.

Camus said it plainly: "Hatred of the creator can turn into hatred of the creation . . . mankind without God brutally wields power."[8]

So Camus's critique of how people confront meaninglessness in an indifferent universe full of plagues doesn't apply just to the broccoli-haired optimist preaching God as the cure for plague. It also extends to the crusty-mustached college bro in a black hoodie—*DawkinsFan99*—who rants about determinism and reposts flying-spaghetti-monster memes from Reddit.

Camus didn't care whether the story came from a pulpit or a podcast. If it tried to explain away the absurd, if it made the silence of the universe sound like a plan, he wasn't buying it. Neither the preacher nor the Reddit atheist gets a pass.

All right, Mr. Internet Atheist. You've made your argument: If God exists, he must be cruel for allowing this plague. But now prepare yourself. Prepare for the gulag. Prepare for the depravity that follows the death of "evil religion." The man-god has arrived, and he offers no more hope for Novemberton than the God he's rejected.

And as I reflect, I can't help but wonder: Doesn't Camus's critique extend just as easily to the activist, the columnist, the celebrity, and the delivery driver? I have every doubt they'll build a more beautiful world. What I fear more is that, in trying, they might create something even uglier than the one they accuse God of failing to fix. Who knows where their optimism might lead, or how quickly their good intentions might rot?

But then again, what if they prove to be good?

If Dostoyevsky has anything to say about it, there's still cause for concern.

The Hero, the Vanguard, the Thinker, the Rebel, they aren't the activist, the columnist, the celebrity, or the delivery driver. But they echo each other. Each, in their own way, follows a human religion.

Their efforts might look like a way forward. But are they? Are they enough to bring anyone closer to the kind of meaning the soul aches for in a cold, unresponsive universe? Are they enough to end the November of the soul?

MORE DAYS OF PLAGUE

The plague didn't stop.

It moved like fog through the town—slow, steady, and without remorse. Taking mothers and a doctor who had just finished his shift.

And the town responded the only way it knew how.

The activist grew louder. The columnist's voice spread farther. The celebrity expanded and thrived. The delivery driver never missed a shift.

They said the plague would run its course soon. The fog would lift. The numbers would flatten. But I didn't believe it, because even if the bacteria died, something else had taken root. They were infected.

So I waited, with that sick, sour feeling that maybe, just maybe, there really was no one left to blame.

And if that was true, if the world really was this empty, this unfeeling, and this closed, then the only thing left was to watch.

Not for the end but for the days ahead. To see how each of them would carry it. What they'd cling to. What they'd abandon. What they'd become beneath the weight of it all.

Chapter Eight

ACTING OUR WAY OUT

The issues at the heart of the culture wars will be decisive for the future . . . and they will have to be settled—but not in the present, destructive manner.

—Os Guinness, *The Cast for Civility*

It's supposed to be a quiet walk. A chance for some air. November stretches on, endlessly, in this town. It's weighing on my soul, but I can't leave. Not yet.

Then I turn a corner and step into a war zone.

Signs wave like spears and voices holler. Before I have a chance to turn around, hands grab me, bodies shove, elbows jab into my ribs. I can hardly breathe as the rage of the crowd pins me against a wall covered in torn posters, all shouting the same fury.

I search for an exit, frantic to get out.

A bottle smashes against a shield as chants turn into screams. A wave of riot police surges forward. I manage to dart away seconds before the pepper spray hits.

I turn to run, then her eyes catch mine.

She stands safely on the side. Searching. I immediately recognize her from the café—the vacant scrolling, the awkward pause. Her gaze burned into my memory. And now here she is again, still uncertain.

The protesters in Novemberton respond to the plague—and the indifferent universe—with the religion of activism. In this belief system, humans center themselves, assuming sole responsibility for creating a fairer, more just world where suffering is diminished and justice prevails. The response to human suffering—and the search for meaning—lies in humanity's ability to forge a promised land.

The concept of the promised land is viewed through two starkly different lenses. The activists believe the world has never been just and that it is humanity's responsibility to shape it into the world it should be, where the promised land awaits in the future. The opposition, however, sees the promised land not ahead of but behind them, a world their grandparents knew, now slipping away. A world they feel compelled to rescue. Though these two sides are diametrically opposed in their vision of the world, they are deeply aligned in their conviction that the answer to the burden of existing in an indifferent universe lies in the fight for, and activism toward, the world they each envision.

THE CULTURE WARS AND NIHILISTIC EXTREMISM

One child. But the horror of his death, an innocent life stolen too soon, has undone everything. What I'm witnessing isn't politics. It's nihilistic extremism wrapped in a culture war. This is the raze craze come to life. Active nihilism unhinged, a flamethrower response to the void. I've seen the memes, the theories, the tribal cries. But this is it in the flesh, fueled by resentment, that festering moral rage that turns helplessness into righteousness. A desperate attempt to alleviate the anxiety caused by the existential vacuum consuming Novemberton as they face the absurdity of the world head on.

All of these thoughts run through my head as I watch her. Her eyes don't burn with the hatred that fuels the others, but I sense the spark, the possibility that they might. She teeters on the edge, tempted by the passionate cries of the culture wars that have swallowed much of Novemberton. Each side pulses with conviction, loud and sure of themselves. In the chaos, that kind of certainty feels like a lifeline.

The ghost at the feast has returned, haunting everyone with a desperate sense of helplessness in an indifferent universe. And the knee-jerk response is to assert one's own power and vision for the world without any deep reflection. It's less about finding a solution and more about reclaiming power.

This is what the culture wars have become in Novemberton—extreme active nihilism dressed up as conviction. The shouting isn't just rage, it's liturgy.

And like any liturgy, it offers a kind of solace—it brings comfort to the worshiper. It becomes familiar and repeatable. A rhythm to follow. But when someone threatens that comfort, the only response is escalation; the activism must intensify to protect the vision. Often, if not always, this leads to extremism and the drive to destroy.

To be clear, not all activism is driven by a desire to destroy. Movements like those for civil rights, women's suffrage, and anti-apartheid were constructive forces aimed at creating positive change and improving society in profound ways.

The extremism brewing in Novemberton, however, is headed toward a destructive clash between two moral visions bent on annihilating one another in a battle over control and power. In this form of activism, negation becomes the dominant mode of engagement—less about development and more about annihilating the other. The key difference is that this sort of activism is nihilistic, stemming from frustration and disillusionment with the world. It seeks disruption instead of meaningful transformation.

At the heart of nihilistic extremism is an aggravated sense of self-preservation—impulsive reactions driven by base instincts—aimed at preserving one's sense of significance to keep from falling into a void of despair. The methods employed in nihilistic extremism are excessive, yet those who use them are so consumed by their disillusionment that even the most extreme tactics seem justified in their eyes. Property destruction, shootings, throwing blood, defecating on national monuments, and vandalizing works of art—these are far removed from the nonviolent protests championed by the civil rights movement.

As Novemberton continues to placate the ghost at the feast, meaningful dialogue disintegrates into nihilistic tribalism. Tribalism is characterized by a deep loyalty to a group that shares a common worldview, often at the expense of those with differing perspectives. Nihilistic tribalism, moreover, emerges from a collective sense of despair, where these tribes are bound not by hope or purpose but by a shared sense of disillusionment and a desire to reject the world as it is.

Novemberton now feels like two cities on opposite sides. Those who refrain from aligning with either side hesitate to admit it, as "sitting in the middle" now seems unreasonable, even spineless. It's seen as indifference, evidence that those in the middle never truly cared about the town or held any genuine values. Ironically, maintaining composure has come to feel like an act of radical defiance.

TOXIC VOIDISM

The clash rises, chants grow louder, people fight back as chaos takes over the streets. Pepper spray hisses, fueling the wrath rather than silencing it. It feels like the protesters mistake rage for redemption.

Suddenly, a bottle explodes nearby. I instinctively duck, covering my face, stumbling backward. My eyes sting from the pepper spray hanging in the air. As I try to find my way out, I notice she hasn't moved.

She's still on the edge of the crowd, untouched, eyes wide with curiosity. The uncertainty that haunted her gaze is gone. She leans slightly forward, like she's ready to make a decision. She's trembling—not with fear but with yearning.

And it all comes together.

She's been scrolling through her days like everyone else in Novemberton, absent and untethered, but the narcotic lull of zettabytes no longer dulls the ache.

Nobody scrolls forever without landing somewhere. Eventually, she had to hit something—some cause, some tribe, some digital prophet whispering meaning into the void.

For a second, I think she's going to step forward.

But she doesn't.

She stays suspended on the side, just long enough for me to wonder whether that small pause is the last thread between her and the ghost. I long for the thread to pull her back, to tether her to something real, but it feels hopeless.

I can't breathe. I don't know whether it's the pepper spray or the protest or the dread of what might happen next.

I finally peel my eyes away from her and manage to find a way to safety. I can't watch any longer; I can't bear to see her consumed by the crowd, swallowed whole by the ghost of nihilism.

The early promise of social media and the digital information boom was an idealistic one: democratized knowledge, a well-informed public, a thriving marketplace of ideas, a place to negotiate meaning. Now, with enough time to measure the long-term effects, reality tells a different story. Social media hasn't enlightened the masses, it has radicalized them, nihilized them. Instead of fostering thoughtful discourse toward a better future, it has become an incubator for extreme ideologies and conspiracy theories. It's not the place where ideas compete, it's where radicals go to breed.

Shaping values and building meaning is slow work. To achieve meaningful transformation, deep reflection is necessary. Thoughtful responses, logic, and critical thinking are required—things that take time. Think of the moments that shaped your deepest convictions. What were they exactly? A father's wisdom. A mother's guidance. A coach who cared enough to visit you at home. A professor who took time to have lunch. A mentor who shared hard-earned insight.

Values don't form in a vacuum, they grow through meaningful relationships and affections—human things. But the digital age has eroded these bonds, replacing them with fleeting online interactions. The result? A generation raised not by mentors passing forward wisdom to people they care about but by algorithms. It's inhuman.

The girl at the café would be better off sitting under the care of a mentor as she searches for meaning. But in the age of zettabytes, people wait for a radical personality to tell them who they are, what they should be, and what it all means. Eventually, an online personality will take hold of her and convert her to the religion of activism, pushing her to find meaning by choosing a side in the culture war. The algorithm now produces disciples, mentored not by wisdom but by hotter and hotter takes in a silo of insanity.

On social media, human nature is suppressed and replaced with cold, hard facts (or supposed facts). What is. What isn't. No wonder extreme activism destroys without flinching. Information is severed from human connection. So cue the trolling. Cue the flaming. Cue the pile-ons. Dox! Cancel! Destroy! Human affections don't matter.

But destruction for the sake of destruction—though posing as activism—doesn't fill the existential void. Cold, hard facts don't stop the plague. Digital detachment and ideological extremism only deepen nihilism, yet those caught in its grip mistake it for meaning. But it's not. It's emptiness masquerading as meaning. The idea that the death of an innocent child could be reduced to a detached, radical agenda driven by a doubling down on "the facts" is both heartbreaking and deeply wrong. I wouldn't even call the religion of activism vibrant voidism. It's toxic voidism.

Is it an attempt to fill the void? Sure. But is it meaningful? Is it human? Does it serve our deepest longings? Not even close. It's a destructive pursuit that only deepens the despair brought on by the plague.

As Os Guiness has said, "The issues at the heart of the culture wars will be decisive for the future . . . and they will have to be settled—but not in the present, destructive manner."[1] We could add to this and say, "Finding meaning during a time of plague is necessary for the future . . . it has to be settled—but not through the religion of nihilistic extremism, tribalism, and toxic voidism, not through the religion of activism." Simply put, entrusting the search for our deepest meaning to the culture wars—and their online sages—is a big mistake. Activism won't get us out of this. It won't secure the promised land.

A CHASING AFTER THE WIND

I'm already halfway down the road, but I can't stop looking back. I see her take a step. My stomach drops. The call of activism—the desperation for meaning—is too much for her to resist.

She steps forward again. Still hesitant.

Then determination kicks in, like a gust of wind filling a sail.

Her steps quicken and her voice joins the protest as she disappears into the crowd. It's like watching a storm swallow the shoreline, pulling the sand into its depths until it becomes part of the sea. The moment leaves me with the sense that she has merged with the masses, perhaps soon to become one of the loudest voices in the crowd. Maybe that's how it started for the activist who first led the charge.

I want to call out, but I don't. I already know it's too late.

Ecclesiastes pierces me with clarity: "Yet when I surveyed all that my hands had done and what I had toiled to achieve, everything was meaningless, a chasing after the wind; nothing was gained under the sun" (Eccl. 2:11).

Action alone doesn't create meaning. Not when it's born of rage. Not when it feeds on fear and validation. That kind of activism, reactive, restless, and hungry, can't resolve the ache it promises to heal.

Consider the Vanguard and his petty stunts: twisting the nose of a harmless old man, kissing another man's wife in public, biting the governor's ear. Each was an attempt to feel something, to carve out meaning. Yet the cold despair of Novemberton never left his soul. For all his spectacle, the void only deepened.

Nihilistic activism is no different. It too is a spectacle, driven by the same restless need to matter, to push against the void with force and noise.

In the end, the girl from the café will find herself just as disillusioned as when she began, just as perplexed, just as hollow as the Vanguard, when all is said and done.

I'm reminded of conversations I've had over the years with students caught in activism. They vary, but they all follow a similar script.

Angrily they book an appointment and tell me how much they hate their country, their peers, and the beliefs they grew up with.

"Do you hate me?" I'll ask.

"Maybe."

"Do you hate yourself?"

"Sometimes, yeah."

There's usually a sharp edge to their words; they don't realize how nihilistic they sound.

I've heard variations of the same story from many students over the years. Their perspectives are shaped, often deeply, by the currents of social media. I've seen them join protests fueled by outrage over injustices in their communities, convinced that their generation is the one to make change. They look back at themselves and laugh, not because it's funny but because they've outgrown that version of themselves. What once felt urgent and life altering now feels naïve.

All that activism, all that outrage, and yet, years later, they're brooding in nihilistic anger. The activism didn't deliver what they hoped. They're no closer to the world they envisioned, no closer to control, no closer to meaning.

Still empty.

The culture war offers no lasting solution. It's a chasing after the wind.

Peter Kreeft, an American philosopher, warns against engaging in these ideological battles. The cure for the plague is not found in identifying an enemy and destroying them, not in hatred. It is not about waging war against every ism you oppose. "All it takes is saints."

This suggests that true meaning requires something deeper than mere action, something more thoughtful than the knee-jerk reactions that dominate the culture wars.

The good news? They are still searching for something beyond the surface, still seeking clarity. That search is no small thing. There they are, in my office, sitting with someone trusted, doing the slow, deliberate work of reflection and formation. Wrestling with the November of their souls, their nihilism, in a space of honest engagement.

WE CAN'T ACT OUR WAY OUT OF THIS

I keep thinking about her, how easy it is for someone to slip from uncertainty into noise. The unbearable immediacy life can sometimes demand. I've felt that pull before.

Albert Camus understood that kind of pressure. He wrote a whole book about it. *The Stranger* begins with Meursault speaking indifferently about his mother's death: "Maman died today. Or yesterday. I don't know."[2] That line isn't just cold, it's a detached confession. Meursault isn't indifferent because he doesn't care, he's overwhelmed by the immediacy of life in a world that offers no guidance, no explanation, no resolution.

Camus doesn't offer moral commentary. In fact, he rejects superhuman solutions to the human condition. He gives us Meursault, observationally honest, emotionally inert, and unmistakably human. A man fully exposed to the absurd, staring into the indifference of the universe with no illusions left to hold on to.

The heat, a consistent motif throughout the novel, becomes the texture of that absurdity. We see it from the inside out. At the beach, as the sun presses in, Meursault begins to fracture: "The sun was starting to burn my cheeks, and I could feel drops of sweat gathering in my eyebrows. The sun was the same as it had been the day I'd buried Maman [Mom], and like then, my forehead especially was hurting me, all the veins in it throbbing under the skin. It was this burning, which I couldn't stand anymore, that made me move forward."[3]

That unbearable discomfort pushes him into action, into the murder of a man. No meaning is given. No system offered. Just heat, pressure, and the moment cracking open: "It occurred to me that all I had to do was turn around and that would be the end of it. But the whole beach, throbbing in the sun, was pressing on my back."[4]

That's how Camus renders the absurd: not as theory but as atmosphere. As the texture of the everyday.

You're sweating. You're squinting. The sun's too bright. You're angry and don't know why.

You pull the trigger. The ghost returns. And then it's too late.

That's what I saw in her, just before she stepped into the crowd. The pressure was building: the heat of ideology, the weight of grief, the digital buzz of a thousand competing truths. All of it pressing on her.

Meursault wasn't driven by hate. He was driven by the ache of indifference—the unbearable tension of living in a world that refuses to give you meaning, no matter how much you ask.

The protest felt the same. The shouting wasn't about change. It was about trying not to dissolve.

Camus said that revolt was the only honest response to the absurd. But revolt requires lucidity, not impulse. Presence, not performance.

And this? This wasn't revolt.

This was Meursault pulling the trigger, not because it solved anything but because the absurd had finally gotten too loud.

Chapter Nine

LAUGHING OUR WAY OUT

If you can't joke about the most horrendous things in the world, what's the point of jokes? What's the point in having humor? Humor is to get us over terrible things.

—Ricky Gervais

I'm trying to put distance between myself and the protest. Shouts still echo in my mind. My eyes burn. My heart won't stop hammering. Then a car sputters behind me, nearly knocking me off my feet as I cross the street.

Déjà vu.

I'm instantly back to November 1st.

Pearl Jam's "Yellow Ledbetter" floats through the air, its guitar licks wrapping around the neighborhood with a sense of longing and uncertainty. Exhaust thickens the street, wrapping around me as the car passes. The music lingers, even after the noise of the engine fades.

As the exhaust dissipates, my body begins to settle. Up ahead, a glowing convenience store comes into view, and parked outside, a red 2010 Ford Fiesta. I recognize the car. The driver who nearly hit me is inside, moving slowly, examining the rows of chips like it's a fine art museum.

Looking through the window, it's clear the delivery driver hasn't noticed me. I can't help but stand and watch, observing as he enjoys a break between customers.

The thought strikes me that a convenience store is a sanctuary for certain types of meh-ists—sacred ground for the passive nihilist, providing brief encounters, inexpensive distractions, and an abundance of immediate pleasures that inject the brain with dopamine with all the accuracy of a high-precision fuel injection system. They are usually a town's busiest clinics for boredom, apathy, and coping. Convenience stores are well-loved parts of the community—just ask people what they think of their local Wawa, Sheetz, or Buc-ee's—they are beloved. The universe may not care that a child just died, and that I might be next, but at least I can make the best of it with a pit stop for a sixty-four-ounce soda.

The delivery driver continues to drift through the aisles mindlessly. He casually scans the magazine rack, stopping at some gamer magazines, examining them with unhurried apathy. He lingers by the coolers, then grabs three energy drinks. Finally, he makes his way to the roller dogs, dresses two of them with onions and mustard, and heads to the counter. He asks for two pouches of nicotine and pays with as much effort as a shrug. Hands full, he nudges open the door and passes me without so much as a glance. Back in his car, he sets the items on the seat next to him, starts the engine, and scrolls through his phone while waiting for the ping of his next delivery.

NUMBED REALISM

I look through the car window, watching the driver inhale his junk food, sip his drink, and browse socials with mustard-covered fingers, and suddenly, I get it: numbed realism. It's when people lose their emotional intensity for living. Every day is approached with resignation, emotional detachment, and psychological drift.

It's the opposite of meeting the absurdity of the world with nihilistic extremism. This is nihilistic surrender—or, more precisely, passive nihilism: a muted resignation, where disconnection becomes the only response to a child clutching his teddy bear on a stretcher. For this kind of meh-ist, the search for meaning comes down to choosing between onions and mustard on a hot dog.

Numbed realism is seeing life in its raw, unfiltered form: rejecting romanticized views and accepting the world as it truly is, not as one imagines it to be. Its purpose is to snap one out of the illusion of false dreams.

I get the feeling, watching the delivery driver guzzle his energy drink, that he has no daydreams about some promised land. He doesn't care about the protests. He's sick of driving past them, seeing both sides drinking their own self-righteous flavor of Kool-Aid. Optimism is the cruelest joke, a misguided plague of its own. Why bother hoping for a better tomorrow in some idealized version of Novemberton? Another plague will hit, corrupt leadership will rise again, kids will die, buildings will crumble, and wars will restart. The cries of injustice will fade into the noise, drowned out by a world that's too caught up in its own tribe's woundedness. Eventually, the sun will explode and none of it will matter anyway. The only real way to respond to the plague is to pull the rug out from under all those hopeful idiots, holding signs and getting pepper sprayed, and remind them just how ridiculous they are.

The delivery driver bites into his hot dog, scrolls through his phone, and finds a photo. He saves it and slots it into a meme template.

I grin; he's making a meme.

He laughs, nearly chokes on his hot dog, and posts it to an account he's somehow in charge of. I glance at the meme. It's dark. So dark it catches me off guard and forces out an involuntary laugh. Somehow I notice the tiniest detail—he has ninety-six followers. That's right, the delivery driver isn't exactly an influencer. His memes go unnoticed, and still every post amuses him.

It is possible he is indifferent to the outcome, unconcerned with feedback. In this case, his memes aren't designed to kick off some grand awakening. He's posting these for his own sake, to laugh. Like his hot dogs and energy drinks, his memes serve as numbing agents to help him face the void—the cold, indifferent universe that doesn't care about the death of a child or the outrage it inspires.

GALLOWS HUMOR

Gallows humor is a dark, sardonic style of comedy that finds laughter in life's bleakest moments. The term comes from the gallows, where condemned prisoners often cracked morbid jokes before their execution.

Examples abound on Reddit, stuff that's shocking. Here's one. Imagine it in a Ricky Gervais accent: "What's the best way to get chewing gum out of your hair? Cancer."

Offended?

Well, the passive nihilist isn't. For two reasons. Gallows humor:

1. *Reflects reality.* The numbed realist accepts the world as it is. Activism, religion, intellectual debates—these are all unrealistic ways to search for meaning. All there is, is what's in front of you. Don't try to figure another way of looking at it. Just deal with it. Whether it's onions on a hot dog or cancer.
2. *Is resistance.* Gallows humor mocks the naïve hope people place in optimistic narratives. It's a quiet acknowledgment of superiority, the strength to accept the world's absurdity. It's like saying, "I see through the illusion."

So gallows humor turns every horrible thing into a punch line and dismantles the comforting ways people find to get to sleep at night. For the delivery driver and his ninety-six followers, it's, ironically, the town's unsung hero.

Consider this. There are a few ways to face the meaninglessness of life:

1. Fight it (the activist).
2. Reason it (the columnist).
3. Take advantage of it (the celebrity).

But the delivery driver and his followers think all of these are naïve. The world is a failed project, crumbling, and effort is pointless.

Gallows humor embodies the only realistic approach: Accept reality at face value (the delivery driver). Let go of illusions like activism, intellectualism, and materialism. They won't save you.

Shows like *It's Always Sunny in Philadelphia*, *Curb Your Enthusiasm*, *BoJack Horseman*, and *Rick and Morty* are packed with gallows humor. Take *Rick and Morty*, for instance. In one episode, Rick and Morty play a virtual reality game called Roy. Morty hooks up to the game, which simulates his life. He starts out as a child with big dreams of becoming a football star—"Roy the Rocket." But as life goes on, he finds himself as a carpet salesman. Then, in his midlife, he's told he has cancer. He beats it, and his close friends and family throw him a party with a banner reading "Cancer Can't Beat the Rocket!" He goes back to selling carpets, smiles at his #1 Dad trophy, and then, while pulling down carpet, he falls off a ladder and dies.

Rick, after watching the simulation, says, "Not bad, Morty. Fifty-five years! But you wasted your thirties with that whole birdwatching thing." He looks at the game's results and adds, "Look at this. You beat cancer and went back to the carpet store—boo!"[1]

This kind of humor can be considered nihilism with a sugar coating: It makes the mood of meaninglessness go down easier by laughing at it. Morty had big dreams, a family, and a trophy, but in the end, it didn't matter. He got cancer, beat it, and died anyway. The universe didn't care.

Rick and Morty critiques how people search for meaning in meaningless things. The meaning they attach to life—like trophies that say "World's #1 Dad" or "Cancer Can't Beat the Rocket!" or whatever purpose birdwatching is supposed to provide—becomes irrelevant in a universe where death can come at any time, indifferent to all their efforts.

You can fight it, overthink it, take advantage of it; you can ignore it. But that won't stop you from falling off a ladder after surviving cancer, if that's what happens. And when it happens, there will always be people who act surprised. They avoid the void, preferring comforting illusions. The best response is to laugh at it. That's all you can really do.

I watch the delivery driver pop in a nicotine pouch and I begin to understand his laughter. His memes, in their ironic way, are the real heroes of this existential plague; they confront reality and make light of existence, much like the creators of *Rick and Morty*. Not that being the hero would matter to the delivery driver, but I imagine he'd appreciate the irony.

EDGELORD: SURRENDER OR PROTEST?

My curiosity gets the best of me. I stroll by the Ford Fiesta and look right into the window. He's so absorbed in his nicotine high and meme making he doesn't even notice me. On the screen, I catch a glance of his Instagram handle: @sinusmilk.

Sinus Milk. So that's what he goes by. Turns out he's been quietly posting his own brand of existential meme content for years. And the last one—the one I just saw him create in his car—might be his darkest yet.

- Image 1 (Vince McMahon intrigued): "Winter fog plague is spreading fast."
- Image 2 (Vince McMahon excited): "It's wiping out the city and taking away comfort and the illusions we cling to!"
- Image 3 (Vince McMahon even more excited): "People are realizing life has no inherent meaning. Everything is futile!"
- Image 4 (Vince McMahon ecstatic): "And it doesn't matter! Nothing matters! Embrace the void!"

I notice he has 3,746 posts; he's been running this account for ages. Sinus Milk is a true edgelord. An edgelord is someone on social media who tries to shock people with dark humor. The name comes from the edge of a sword—sharp, extreme, cutting, and painful.

An edgelord doesn't fit neatly into a category.

On one hand, they could be a meh-ist, posting memes for the same reason an artist might put their feces in a can and call it art, or a Slipknot fan dresses in black, or the woman on the talk show tells everyone she's not having kids. It's all the same: They don't care. They surrender to the plague as it flattens them.

But what if I've misread him? What if Sinus Milk isn't a passive nihilist at all? What if these memes are a form of protest? Maybe he's not indifferent to the plague. Maybe he's trying to kick-start something. Maybe he's mocking the way people make meaning during the plague.

In that case, the memes aren't a total abandonment of hope, even if they seem that way at first. He's responding to the cold universe in shocking ways to create new values. He's not just opting out of activism, intellectualism, and material indulgence. He's protesting against FOMO. There's no promised land to fear missing out on, one that activism, material indulgence, and intellectualism could provide. And the same could be said of the Slipknot fan, the artist creating with feces, and the woman who thinks a bulk jar of mayonnaise from a warehouse is a better investment than having a child. This is vibrant voidism in a darker form: protesting the idea that values offer any real hope in unrealistic narratives.

Thus, meh-ism and vibrant voidism are similar, separated only by motivation. So when your kids post 9/11 memes and you think they're total nihilists, it might be true, but they might also be reevaluating their values. Maybe they're grieving in meme form. Maybe they've realized that promised lands don't exist—not when innocent people are forced to jump out of buildings or children aren't able to see the otters at the zoo.

METAMODERNISM

For the sake of argument, let's assume Sinus Milk isn't just some shrugging meh-ist but something more. Let's say those 3,746 memes were posted not out of apathy but out of protest. Not loud, dramatic protest. Meme protest. Absurdity-as-resistance protest.

In that case, we could say he is "metamodern."

Metamodernism is a cultural mood that tries to build value again, without pretending the world isn't a mess. It's not overly optimistic like modernism, which clung to progress, science, and grand narratives. (Remember how all that ended . . . ehm, World War II and A-bombs, ehm.) And it's not cynical like postmodernism, which rolled its eyes at truth and deconstructed everything until nothing was left.

Metamodernism is both. It oscillates.

Metamodernism holds the optimism of modernity in tension with the critique of postmodernism, aiming to create meaning that's neither overly optimistic nor totally pessimistic.

It hopes with a wink. It laughs at the absurdity of life. It memes the plague. But it doesn't lose track of the fact that things in the present still matter, such as getting people their fast food on time so that hungry people in a plague can eat.

A meme, if posted with protest in mind, is metamodern because the serious content—a plague killing people—conflicts with the medium it's delivered through—a set of goofy Vince McMahon images. It balances darkness and humor, pushing past modernity's optimistic narratives and postmodernity's cynical deconstruction.

It says, "Hey, life is my ranch sauce. Because that's all I have now. I'm going to enjoy the sweet goodness of dipping my buffalo wings into it, without deconstructing how cruel it is to kill chickens or believing that ranch sauce will cure the plague." It accepts that too many buffalo wings could lead to high cholesterol and heart attacks, but also accepts that there's no better ten minutes of joy in life than the crunch of a deep-fried wing.

In essence, metamodernism is about focusing on what's right in front of you for what it is—the good, the bad, and the ugly—without too much construction or deconstruction, whether it's chicken wings, a plague, or the death of a child.

WHO WANTS TO MEET SINUS MILK?

In one of my philosophy classes, we dissected the enigma of Sinus Milk—ambiguously numbed, metamodern, teetering between vibrant voidism and meh-ism. It was, without a doubt, the funniest lecture I ever taught. We imagined him until he almost felt real, standing right in front of us. Then I asked, "Who wants to meet this guy?" One student responded, "If he was my delivery driver, I'd order from him every night!"

The class said he'd probably be the coolest hang. They'd tip him extra just to hear him drone on about whatever was on his mind. Some thought he'd have the best hot takes imaginable. They appreciated his sincerity, his honesty, his willingness to toss out unreasonable optimism and pessimism. They admired his courage to dress himself in a jumbo hot dog and eat it while the plague ravaged the town.

Then I asked, "How many here want to be Sinus Milk?"

The laughing subsided.

Nobody.

We talked about this for a while, soberly. It wasn't just his distasteful pleasantries and odd BO, which we all agree smelled like baked underwear. In spite of his sincerity, there was something unsettling about hope that doesn't go beyond a convenience store, beyond a meme that calls to just the here and now. Sure, the delivery driver's sincerity might be admirable, but hope in ranch sauce still leaves people adrift. That veers too close to nihilism and will always feel closer to hopelessness, even if it's trying to construct authentic values without despair.

Perhaps that's why the edgelord, the vibrant voidist, is always confused with a meh-ist: Their motives, though noble, still can't offer any values that make an indifferent world feel less unforgiving or meaningless. It all feels the same, whether surrendering to the void or fighting it off with a dank meme.

I watch the delivery driver relish the remnants of his caffeine and nicotine buzz, and think back to the Hero from the panel discussion. He too wavered between nihilism and constructed conviction, caught in the pendulum swing. The Hero tried to will purpose into being, to become the author of his own salvation. But the strain broke him. In the end, he cashed out with nothing but despair.

When one tries to find meaning through self-will in a world without God—whether through suicide, memes, or ranch sauce—the self-will is bound to crack under the weight. The tension between nihilism and meaning making eventually collapses, and no amount of irony or deflection can shield against the suffocating reality of existence. There's no convincing you that the delivery driver, in the end, will find more peace than the Hero. You can't numb yourself enough to escape the plague forever. Eventually, realism, gallows humor, passive surrender, and protest falter; none can hold up against the weight of an indifferent universe.

Sinus Milk's phone buzzes. A delivery order comes in.

He crumples up his wrappers, throws them into the back seat, and sputters away. I watch the hero of the town drive into the night to supply the hungry people of Novemberton with both fast food and memes. I can't help but wonder how long he will be able to laugh in order to keep from crying.

Chapter Ten

INDULGING OUR WAY OUT

I am the master of my fate; I am the captain of my soul.

—William Ernest Henley, "Invictus"

Don't say I never did anything for the plague," she laughs, lifting a glass.

"One million dollars raised for the relief fund. And—drumroll, please—three million live viewers tonight!"

She blows kisses to the camera. Makes heart hands to the crowd and her online viewers.

"It was terrifying to be stuck here during the plague, but my motto has always been to make the most of every moment; write your own story, right?"

The room erupts in applause.

I'm seated in a dark corner, slightly removed from the circus. My mustard scarf doesn't quite cut the dress code. Someone hands me a drink I haven't asked for, and I take it without thinking—hoping it makes me look more like I belong. I'm still not sure why security waved me in.

Just before this, I was standing beneath the buzzing lights of the convenience store. My thoughts were circling, spinning—round and round in the hollow ache of Novemberton. November never ends here. It stretches cold and gray across every street and hour of the day. Like so many other days, I began walking, piecing together answers. I must have walked for miles. I heard the music first, then the air filled with laughter. It made me stop dead in my tracks.

A party? In Novemberton?

That's when I saw the spotlights and the manor. I don't know what possessed me to walk up. But I did. And they let me in.

Guests in designer suits and evening gowns with champagne flutes in hand covered the grounds. Gatherings are still forbidden in Novemberton, but no one here cared. That's when I followed the crowd inside and sat down in the corner to watch her performance.

Still stunned by what she said, I look around and begin to feel the shape of the truth forming. I see tripods with ring lights fill the house, each holding a smartphone. A few plainly dressed workers weave between them, adjusting angles and monitoring streams. In the living room, the celebrity who had been filming in Novemberton before the plague began stands at the center of a captivated crowd, everyone fawning over her speech and the gala.

I notice that each camera frames her newly launched activewear line. For "tonight only," all sales will support plague victims.

I can't help but feel like the entire gala is tone deaf. It seems the celebrity is exploiting the plague—and the tragic death of an innocent child—as a means to push her brand, gain product exposure, and bolster her credibility. And everyone surrounding her? They're seizing the opportunity to boost their own clout and increase their social capital.

FORCES THAT FUEL THE INDIVIDUAL SOUL

One way to find meaning in a world without God is through individualism. Individualism is the belief that meaning and purpose are self-determined, where each person defines their own reality and prioritizes their autonomy. For an individualist, the quest for meaning becomes a personal responsibility: One must determine what brings fulfillment and choose how to live. You are responsible to yourself.

William Ernest Henley's 1875 poem "Invictus" describes the search for meaning through individualism. It reflects on a personal plague of his own: a battle with tuberculosis and the amputation of his leg. The poem expresses defiance against both his physical pain and the potential meaninglessness of the circumstances. It asserts that meaning is something one must create for oneself, in spite of the cards one is dealt:

> Out of the night that covers me,
> Black as the pit from pole to pole,
> I thank whatever gods may be
> For my unconquerable soul.
>
> In the fell clutch of circumstance
> I have not winced nor cried aloud.
> Under the bludgeonings of chance
> My head is bloody, but unbowed.
>
> Beyond this place of wrath and tears
> Looms but the Horror of the shade,
> And yet the menace of the years
> Finds and shall find me unafraid.
>
> It matters not how strait the gate,
> How charged with punishments the scroll,
> I am the master of my fate,
> I am the captain of my soul.[1]

Many who aren't familiar with "Invictus" often recognize its famous closing lines: "I am the master of my fate, / I am the captain of my soul." As an individualist, Henley insists that he alone controls his destiny, not divine intervention or any external force. It's within him to define his purpose, find fulfillment, and determine the meaning of his life.

A lesser known part of the poem is where Henley acknowledges "whatever gods may be." In this, he's not bowing to a traditional deity but rather acknowledging the impersonal forces in life that fuel one's willpower to create meaning out of life. This sentiment often pops up on social media: Picture someone on vacation, soaking in the sun on the Greek Isles, surrounded by friends and posting something like "forces that fuel my soul."

These "forces," or as Henley calls them, "gods," are the sources of strength and fulfillment that empower individuals to continue forging their own paths, guiding them as the captains of their own souls, creating their own meaning along the journey.

PRACTICAL POLYTHEISM

The party carries on, all laughter and shimmer, and it strikes me that the forces giving meaning to attendees' lives in spite of the plague are influence, social capital, and even their misguided sense of altruism. They believe they're helping others, when in truth they're mostly helping themselves.

I watch the party unfold like it's in slow motion—duck-face selfies, champagne toasts, group hugs, camera flashes—happy people basking in the glow of doing what makes them feel good. Maybe all of this performative joy masks a quiet desperation. A need for a god of some kind, just one dressed in filters and flattery, unnoticed even by those who worship.

At the heart of the gala, beneath the layers of ambition and altruism, might be the group's attempt to respond to their own philosophical void with such a god.

They have a felt need—a need for meaning. The plague has exposed the gaps in the way they make that meaning.

Innocence stolen by the plague. The weighty thought of death. The inescapable shadow of mortality. Will anyone remember them? And so the gala becomes a platform to serve the "I"—the need for something significant, something lasting, like building a brand or influence that outlives oneself.

As I watch their movements, it feels less like an event to help the sick or build a brand and more like a kind of religious gathering, a ceremony in which they soothe their existential anxiety. Gods such as relevance, success, beauty, and belonging reign here. Not as eternal deities but as immediate ones. Ones that are tangible, streamable, on brand.

In my class, I began to call this "practical polytheism." Not polytheism in the traditional sense, like the worship of statues or spirits, but in the subtle turn toward anything that promises to meet a felt need.

The concept came to me while researching for this book. I surveyed theology professors with a simple prompt: Finish this sentence: "In a world without God . . ."

There were many insightful answers, but one stood out: "In a world without God, there are many gods."

This answer echoes Henley's view: In a world without God, the gaps exposed by the indifferent universe are filled by anything—any force—that serves the individual self. People become open to whatever can provide what they need, and what they need *now.*

Practical polytheism becomes the act of seeking fulfillment by turning to various forces that serve immediate needs. It hinges on our feelings, on interpreting our emotional states and filling the gaps with the forces we crave.

In practical polytheism, things are flipped. Individuals don't serve gods, but the gods serve them. Meaning becomes whatever satisfies personal desire. Yet one of life's ironies is how often we're harmed by the very gods we chase.

Consider the example of the social-media adult star who engaged with 101 partners in a single day, only to break down afterward, describing the experience as "robotic." This attempt to fill the emptiness with a force—or god—collapses because it is devoid of a solid, sustainable foundation. Giving meaning to your life by filling the gaps with gods offers only temporary relief, and the underlying frustration is inevitable.

Her tears and her feeling of being "robotic"—dehumanized in her own act—point to a greater truth: Forces beyond our control, and even beyond the gods we turn to, undermine the power of these gods. They are not as capable as we might think.

This tension between individualism and its darker consequences is palpable when we turn to Henley's famous poem, which is often celebrated for its empowering message of meaning making. Yet it's unsettling to realize that this poem was the final statement of one of the most notorious killers in American history: Timothy McVeigh, who was executed in 2001 for the Oklahoma City bombing in 1994. McVeigh carried out the bombing as an act of revenge against the federal government, motivated by what he perceived as abuses of power during incidents like Ruby Ridge and Waco. His violent rebellion was his attempt to assert meaning through his individualism, his attempt at significance.

From my seat, the room no longer feels bright, the guests no longer sparkle; it all feels haunted. I replay the figures in my mind—the celebrities and influencers at the gala, the Rebel at the panel discussion. Both are deeply engaged with their pursuit of purpose and fulfillment. The Rebel, while radical, is still an individualist in the truest sense, as his quest for filling the gaps rests on his personal prerogative. Similarly, the influencers, though not violent, channel their individualism through their own personal prerogative.

No one is promoting violence like the Rebel, but the connection is still stark: The pursuit of meaning through individualism can lead to devastating consequences. What begins as a search for personal significance may ultimately spiral into destruction and more despair. The gods we use to fill the gaps destroy us.

THE GODS OF THE GAPS

The adult star's tears and McVeigh's alienation stand as stark witnesses against the illusion of absolute individualism. They cry out that human beings cannot simply act on their desires to fill the emptiness within. The human soul resists this; it will not be satisfied by individual attempts at meaning alone. Take the Rebel's example: His grief, paranoia, and psychological unraveling reveal that the gods we create to fill the void of our existential longing are no gods at all. They lack the power to overcome the deeper afflictions that plague us.

Ironically, the title of Henley's poem, "Invictus," means "invincible."

In the book of Judges, the people "did what was right in their own eyes," acting according to their personal quests for meaning and fulfillment. This reflects a form of individualism, where each person or tribe was led by their own desires. Notably, they weren't without gods. They were polytheistic in a traditional sense, turning to idols that promised to meet their felt needs—fertility, prosperity, and protection (Judg. 2:11, 13). In serving these idols, however, the people believed the idols, in turn, served them, offering immediate rewards for their devotion.

But the gods they served made them anything but invincible. As a result of their idolatry, the Israelites:

1. Became slaves to Cushan-Rishathaim (3:8)
2. Became slaves to Eglon, the king of Moab (3:12–14)
3. Were oppressed by Jabin, the king of Canaan (4:2–3)
4. Were oppressed by the Philistines (13:1)
5. Got involved in a civil war that threatened the tribe of Benjamin (19:22–30)

Moreover:

1. Gideon's idolatry led to Israel's national destruction (8:33–35).

2. Abimelech's idolatry led to violence and his own death (9:1–57).
3. Samson's idolatry led to his ruin (16:1–31).
4. Micah's idolatry led to devastation (17–18).
5. The Levites' idolatry led to a concubine's death (19).

The narrative of Judges teaches that the personal quest for meaning and purpose, pursued through the gods of the gaps, ultimately comes at a steep price.

In a way, the book of Judges has parallels with the show *Breaking Bad*, a show widely acclaimed by audiences.

Walter White, once a high school chemistry teacher, lived a modest life until a terminal cancer diagnosis pushed him toward desperation. Determined to provide for his family, he sought control over his fate. His expertise enabled him to figure out how to create a pure kind of meth, making him rich, but his wealth didn't make him invincible. He faced gangs, the cartel, and the police. In the end, he collapsed in his lab, fatally shot, staring at the product of his own unchecked individualism—an empire built, and destroyed, by his own hands. The scene of White's lifeless body in his lab, where he created all that meth, stands as a stark reminder that individualism often leads to ruin.

FRIGHTED BY A CHESTNUT TREE

I'm exhausted, ready to leave, but nobody else is slowing down. The party pulses with the energy of a champagne rush straight to the brain. A guest stumbles into a table, a chair cushioning his fall as he crashes to the ground. Laughter erupts around him. Still in high spirits, the man pauses on the floor, momentarily stunned by his misstep, eyes drifting into the distance.

It seems like he's staring at one of the phones set up with a ring light around it. It looks like a moment meant for a reset, but I wonder whether his drunkenness has cracked something open, an existential honesty that slips through when alcohol lowers your inhibition.

His nausea and vacant stare remind me of a book, Jean-Paul Sartre's *Nausea*. In one of the book's more famous scenes, the protagonist, Roquentin, experiences an existential moment of despair while staring at the root of a chestnut tree from a park bench. As he observes it, Roquentin becomes overwhelmed by nausea. The sickness strikes when the world around him, and the things in it, begin to feel foreign. It's as if the world is announcing itself as strange, and he feels like a foreigner in an odd land.

> So I was in the park just now. The roots of the chestnut tree were sunk in the ground just under my bench. I couldn't remember it was a root anymore. The words had vanished and with them the significance of things . . . I was sitting, stooping forward, head bowed, alone in front of this black, knotty mass, entirely beastly, which frightened me . . . It left me breathless.[2]

Roquentin continues, eloquently detailing how the root of the tree exemplifies the world's inherent meaninglessness. Even words, he writes, are arbitrary, describing things that lack inherent purpose. They convey what things are—what people interpret them to be—but fail to offer grounded significance.

Maybe, just maybe, this man is having his chestnut tree moment, staring at the narcotic light of the cell phone and feeling the nausea of his existence. Reeling. Overwhelmed by the worthlessness of it all. Fame, possessions, social capital—is there purpose in any of it?

The gods of the gaps may serve us momentarily, but they can never fill the one need that everyone seems to seek: lasting significance.

There will always come a moment in the practice of practical polytheism when one takes inventory of one's possessions, bestowed by the gods of the gaps, with the same profound scrutiny as Roquentin's encounter with the tree. The result will be nausea. In these moments, individualism surrenders to the indifferent universe. It will always be frightening.

One of the more fascinating figures who has embarked on his own existential quest for meaning is Jim Carrey. In 1994 alone, he released *Ace Ventura: Pet Detective*, *The Mask*, and *Dumb and Dumber*. Kids in the neighborhood idolized him, constantly quoting lines from his movies: "Allll righty then!" Carrey skyrocketed to fame in the mid-'90s, becoming one of Hollywood's most iconic actors, a title he still holds today.

But today, Carrey is a different man: a more philosophical version of the comedian we all know and love. He has openly shared his reflections in interviews, including this thought-provoking statement: "I think everybody should get rich and famous and do everything they've ever dreamed of so they can see it's not the answer."

His honesty echoes what celebrities like Brad Pitt, Justin Bieber, Ellen DeGeneres, and Dave Chappelle have said about materialism: The gods of the gaps don't make us invincible, they leave us empty, depressed, and drained. Like Roquentin staring at a chestnut tree, in moments of truth, we're left asking, "What's it all for?" with a sense of nausea.

The man at the gala is helped to his feet by friends, who promptly place another drink in his hand. Laughter erupts again as the look of concern fades from his face. He returns to the group, now fully immersed in the performance, pushing the product line and raising money to stop the plague.

I have a feeling the party will stretch into the early hours. Will any of these guests pause for a moment of reflection? Will they question whether their approach to the plague—built on individualism and materialism—can truly fill the gnawing emptiness inside? A deeper hunger calls, one that the gods of the gaps can never satisfy.

As I make my exit, the guests rush to the other side of the manor just in time for the grand finale. Fireworks explode above the estate. The sky, for once, is lit. The brightest Novemberton has seen in ages.

But this light doesn't last. It awes but quickly disappears. If it could reach behind their designer dresses and expensive smiles, it would illuminate hollow spaces no gods can fill.

I burrow into my coat and wait for my taxi to arrive. In the distance, the last burst of color fades into smoke. Then it starts, that familiar rhyme, reverberating in my mind. My stomach churns, the lines' repetition relentlessly nauseating.

> Here we go round the prickly pear
> Prickly pear, prickly pear
> Here we go round the prickly pear
> At five o'clock in the morning.

— Chapter Eleven —

A WAGER ON TRANSCENDENCE

Is it true, prince, that you once declared that "beauty would save the world"?

—Fyodor Dostoyevsky, *The Idiot*

There's a moment after every illusion ends when the silence feels louder than the noise ever did.

That's where I am now. In a car, windows fogged, the outside world blurring past, listening to a voice I barely know.

The columnist.

During my time here, I've rolled my eyes at his broadcasts—his fervor, his sharp commentary on the plague, his tangents. But tonight, something's different. He's not speaking theory. He's speaking grief. Not the loud kind that wails and tears its clothes. The quiet kind that curls itself around you and waits. The kind that makes it hurt to breathe.

My driver doesn't say much. He watches the road, half listening, maybe, or just enjoying the noise. Every now and then, he shifts in his seat, unmoved, like someone who's heard it all before.

On the radio, the columnist's room sounds surprisingly hostile. I can hear it, hissing, heckling interruptions that build until the air is thick with scorn.

Suddenly, his voice cuts through all of it: "For the sake of our happiness—despite what science and tragedy dictate—we must choose to believe in God, even in the absence of evidence. We must wager on transcendence."

The room explodes. Boos. Laughter. Dismissive scoffs.

The driver lets out a laugh: "It's been a while since Novemberton's done that," he mutters, and glances at me in the rearview mirror and shrugs. "This guy, I tell ya." But I don't laugh. I'm too tired, weighted under it all.

The columnist continues. He doesn't offer science, nor does he argue from evidence. He's full of insistence. A desperation not to collapse beneath what he calls "high-altitude thinking"—that cold, mechanical optimism that says humans can face death like gods.

He tells us he's traveled the world and seen what happens when that pride collapses. "And," he says, "it does collapse."

Then, more fiercely, his voice almost trembling with disgust, "I am horror struck at the perception of the poison power of that vapor which strikes with suffocating fumes to the heart of those who enter the school of the atheistic doctrine."[1]

As he speaks, my mind drifts, not away from his words but into them. Into the town. The faces I've seen. The activist's fire turning into fury. The influencer, lit by screens, dancing around her emptiness. The delivery driver, nodding at nothing, headphones on. The IT guy, saving drafts that no one reads. They're not fine. None of them.

A child has died. Their town is breaking. The plague has stripped the distraction away, leaving everyone to face whatever gods they've built for themselves, and it doesn't work.

"The world," the columnist says, "is shattered and shivered, by the hand of atheism, into innumerable glittering quicksilver globules of individual personalities . . . coalescing and parting asunder without unity, coherence, or consistency."[2]

I close my eyes and see their faces. Their eyes. Hollow. Hungering. Haunted. And at that moment, I don't care whether he's right or wrong. I just know he's not lying.

BELIEVING DOESN'T SOLVE THE SCIENTIFIC DILEMMA

The columnist's voice holds steady, even as the room turns against him. He's not surprised. Believing in God doesn't solve the scientific dilemma, and he knows it.

Still, truth demands evidence. The universe remains unmoved by human hope. Even if Novemberton reopened St. Bartholomew's for Mass, the next death—the next child—would crack it all again. The mind would recoil, and faith would start to feel like myth. The columnist doesn't argue with that. He doesn't need to.

He continues.

While modernity cannot reconcile God with zettabytes of data or hold faith within its architecture, it also cannot survive without him. That's the crisis. The town tries to live without belief, and it fails—not for lack of intelligence but because human souls cannot bear what follows. Without God, "wounds will not be healed," he says. "There is no healing hand."[3] This is not a case for God's existence. It's a case for ours.

He's not asking people to believe because it's easy. He's showing that to live without faith is a greater impossibility. Novemberton has proven it: People scroll, protest, curate, theorize, yet none can shoulder the void. They fracture. They pretend. They search for meaning in noise and novelty. But the weight remains.

Without transition, his voice shifts. He tells us about his little son, that first victim of the plague.

After the funeral, he and his wife went to the zoo. They had promised their son they would take him to see the otters. But when they arrived, he couldn't make it past the glass. His wife wept beside him. And in that moment, the philosophy he had studied turned against him. It had no language for that kind of loss, denying the hope that he might one day see his son again and hold him the way his son had clutched his teddy bear.

"Don't humans have a right to joy? A right to hope?" he says. "Hoping for what is eternal, what heals and reconciles, is human! Why repress it in the name of abstract principles and premises given to us by modernity? A life without this hope is unbearable! Should I have spoken of Hume, Nietzsche, Feuerbach, and Chernyshevsky while holding my wife's shaking hands? To do so would be the crudest cowardice!"

Then, as if prompted by the thought itself, there is a clatter—a gasp, sharp as torn paper. Porcelain striking porcelain with a brittle clink, tea spilling out among the rustle of paper. His voice catches, broken, somewhere between pain and apology.

I imagine him before me, tea steaming on the table, dripping onto notes, soaking into what was supposed to be a controlled moment. A symbol, maybe, of all the comforts that no longer hold.

And something in me breaks open.

It's no longer just his story I'm hearing. It's my own. The grief has landed. And it opens something in me I've been holding shut since I arrived.

Not as commentary. Not as theory. As memory.

When I was younger, a friend of mine had a brother, only nineteen, who had aggressive cancer. One evening, I visited my friend's home, and her brother was there. Eagerly, he awaited the arrival of a video game from the UPS driver. He told me how each day, he would sit in his bedroom, looking out the window, waiting for the delivery. Two days after that evening, the young man passed away.

I visited the family, and my friend said, "The hardest part of all this was when we came home from the hospital and saw a package sitting at the door."

She wept bitterly, hoping this wasn't the end of the story.

She needed more than what the world offered. And in this moment, listening to the columnist, I am more certain than ever that I do too.

The fire never left me. It only dimmed. Smothered under the weight of loss and sorrow. But in Novemberton, it has stirred again, faint yet steady—not in argument, not in vision, but in grief.

The fate of the soul is bound to the hope that the universe might still be open, to God, to immortality, to something beyond decay. Even the most hardened skeptic can't bear otherwise. Not when it's someone they love. Not when it's their own.

The columnist speaks again, choking back tears. "But let the disbeliever of immortality imagine a life of sixty minutes instead of sixty years, and let him try if he can bear to see loved, noble, or wise men only aimless, hour-long air phantoms, hollow, thin shadows which fly toward the light, are consumed by it, and who, without patch, trace, or aim, after a short flight, dissolve into their former night."[4]

Then, louder, clearer, "No! Even over him steals a supposition of immortality, the belief in divine transcendence . . . no matter how invisible the God or how unforgiving the plague!"[5]

He's not asking for sentiment. He's naming the cost of its absence.

THE NEW THINKERS

The columnist makes a sobering point: Both religious and nonreligious lives are haunted by the same ghost. Beneath the modern mood, under the weight of meaninglessness, people are torn between modern disenchantment and the possibility of transcendence. The intellect insists that transcendence is a relic. But the soul gnaws for God.

The driver hasn't said anything in a while. His posture, though, has changed. He's less casual, as if the words are taking hold.

And maybe it's not just him. Maybe part of secular society, burdened by infobesity and disillusionment, is quietly losing faith in its own unbelief. The bold certainty of the mid-2000s—Hitchens, Dawkins, Dennett, Harris—feels brittle now. The Four Horsemen rode hard, but the terrain beneath them has shifted.

I think of the New Thinkers—Tom Holland, Douglas Murray, Louise Perry, Jonathan Haidt, Ayaan Hirsi Ali, John Vervaeke, Jordan Peterson. They are evidence of this changing tide. They've watched the confidence of secular humanism crack, watched the fallout: despair, fragmentation, chaos. They ask whether we can really move forward without something sacred. Without roots. Without a story.

I've seen it too—on the panel, in the driver's eyes, in the IT guy's empty stare. Without a fixed point, people drift. Then they drown.

The columnist, in his way, makes the same claim. That even without full commitment to its dogma, we must wager on transcendence. Sigmund Freud said it plainly: Modern Western people suffer not because they're wrong but because they're alone. And Nietzsche saw it coming. Without God, the void opens. Most people can't climb out. Not even the best can will themselves to power. And society starts to rot. The columnist's answer? Return to the fixed. To sacred order. To moral law not invented by men.

And I get it. I look at Novemberton, and it's clear: Everyone is doing what's right in their own eyes. And none of it is working.

"Thou shalt" dissolved in the acid bath. And what did we get? Not freedom. Collapse. The man-God made himself a slave to meaninglessness. Technology soared. The soul stalled.

"For the sake of happiness and liberty," the columnist says, "Novemberton must abandon its high-altitude thinking and believe again. Wager on transcendence and live. Or reject it and decay."

As the driver and I continue, I think back to what seems like a small moment now. A moment on a plane.

We were seated next to each other in the bulkhead row, that coveted section of the cabin where the seats are supposedly special. And by special, I mean they have a few extra inches of legroom and a seatbelt so thick it looks like it was designed for asteroid impact. Seriously, why is it so big? Is it supposed to double as a harness in zero gravity? Nobody knows. But it's wrapped in leather, which gives it the false sense of luxury, like you're about to take a spin in a high-end SUV, not a plane.

Anyway, this woman next to me pulled out her Bible and started highlighting verses, radiating so much joy and contentment that I half expected her to burst into song. She had that glow—the kind that can light up an entire cabin or power a small town. She greeted the flight attendants with genuine kindness and a warm smile. And as we started taxiing down the runway, she buckled in and said with a cheerful grin, "Well, I guess the good Lord gave us these seatbelts for extra protection."

Naturally, I couldn't help myself. I turned to her, laced my voice with maximum snark, and said, "I guess he likes us better than everyone else on the plane?" Her smile froze. You could almost hear her mental gears grind to a halt as she processed the little philosophical grenade I'd just rolled into her lap. For a second, I had her. I could feel the logical structure wobbling.

And then she did the unthinkable. She smiled again—gently, genuinely. Those impossibly forgiving eyes met mine, and she laughed—laughed—at herself. She excused her ignorance. And then turned right back to her Bible and kept highlighting, as if nothing had happened.

Meanwhile, I spent the entire flight sitting there with my arms crossed, stewing. How could someone believe something so naïve? And worse—how could she be so unbothered by having her belief challenged?

As the flight wore on, I started to feel something in me shift. Conviction. Not the religious kind but the kind that makes you realize something uncomfortable: She was probably the kindest, calmest, most gracious person on that plane, and I was likely the most irritable and restless one. A walking bundle of neuroses, on edge.

Maybe life, and what's truly good for a society, isn't served best by the cold, mechanical logic of philosophical arguments. After all, I can't imagine a town full of people like me would be better than one full of people like her. It made me pause and think that human life is far more complex than anything that can be neatly solved with words and reason. There's something about the act of believing in transcendence that feels inherently human, even if it doesn't always fit into a logical framework. It's as though there's a dimension to life that simply can't be reduced to reason alone.

THE BODY OF THE DEAD CHRIST IN THE TOMB

As the silence deepens between the driver and me, the columnist's voice cracks open again. The grief that's been there all along is now speaking without disguise. It leads him to a memory, to a painting.

He tells the audience how it happened years ago, while he was reporting in Basel. On a quiet afternoon, with time to wander, he entered the Kunstmuseum Basel without expectation, to browse its collection of European masters. He found himself frozen before one of its most haunting works: *The Body of the Dead Christ in the Tomb*, painted by Hans Holbein between 1521 and 1522.

He doesn't describe it as a painting at first. He describes it as a collapse. "The whole form is emaciated. The ribs and bones plain to see. Hands and feet riddled with wounds, all blue and swollen, like a corpse on the point of decomposition. The face is too fearfully agonized. The eyes half open still, but with no expression in them, and giving no idea of seeing. Nose, mouth and chin are blue. The whole thing bears a strong resemblance to a real dead body."[6]

He pauses, then quietly adds, "While glaring at it, I thought a man's faith might be ruined by looking at that painting!"[7] He says it not in contempt but in awe.

There is no halo. No radiance. No lingering beauty. Holbein painted Jesus not as a divine figure suspended in suffering but as a man. Dead. Laid in a narrow tomb, rotting. His mouth slack, his eyes frozen open. The painting was likely intended as part of a Holy Sepulcher, a devotional work. And yet it is one of the most disturbing images ever created.

Holbein had grown up shaped by *devotio moderna*, a spiritual tradition that urged believers not to contemplate Christ's suffering from a distance but to enter it. To martyr themselves emotionally by meditating on his broken flesh. Not to be comforted by his godhood but to be undone by his humanity—to feel the guilt of it and still not look away. There are no mourning saints around this Christ, only the body. The wound. The horror.

And that, the columnist says, is what shattered him.

"This was the presentment of a poor mangled body which had evidently suffered unbearable anguish even before its crucifixion, full of wounds and bruises, marks of the violence of soldiers and people, and of the bitterness of the moment when he had fallen with the cross—all this combined with the anguish of the actual crucifixion."[8] And yet even in death, the columnist suggests, it looked as if it still "quivered with agony."

He remembers staring at it and asking, "Supposing the disciples saw this tortured body; how could they have gazed upon the dreadful sight and yet believed that he would rise again?"

The room on the radio is silent. You can almost hear him breathing.

Then he continues, not as a philosopher anymore but as a father. "Holbein's *Dead Christ* is the modern image of God—a God dead in the acid bath. It is the surrender to despair. The cold realism of a universe without comfort. And now I ask, Is this what I'm to believe about my son? The little boy who only wanted to see the otters?"

His voice falters. "Am I to picture him as tortured, frightened, and consumed by the agony of mind and heart? Left in some modern tomb of nothingness? No. I refuse!"

He raises his voice, not in rage but in desperation: "Only if the God of the acid bath escapes, only if he rises, can my son follow him! I have a right to hope! Because I am human, and something in me stretches beyond the grave! My soul dares to wager—to wager that reason is a flickering lantern, and that beyond its reach lies something more enchanted than the harsh realism of an unforgiving universe!"

He chokes back tears, crying, "So take your premises, your logic, your airtight arguments—your God, dissolved in the acid bath! I will wager on hope, while you delight that damn ghost with your hollow abstractions! But if the plague ever takes your son, then you will see. Then your soul will cry out what a cruel logician you are!"

His voice trembles, exhausted now. "I stake everything on hope. Because only a risen God can hold my son again. And it is that hidden beauty, the one that Holbein dares us to imagine on the other side of the tomb, that shall save Novemberton."

The car is still moving, but I don't feel it anymore. The driver's eyes flash to mine in the rearview mirror again. This time they glisten not with reason but with a silent, glassy reverence. A single tear rolls down his cheek.

"It's been a while," he whispers, "since Novemberton's heard something like that."

Then, without warning, he turns right down a quiet, empty street.

"Where are we going?" I ask.

He doesn't answer right away.

Just says, "Somewhere quieter."

— Chapter Twelve —

A STAINED-GLASS REFLECTION

I knew immediately what I was giving up for Lent this year. Atheism. It won't be hard because my atheism has waned in recent years anyway.

—Giles Coren, journalist for *The Times*

We drive through the town. Storefronts, streetlamps, outlines of buildings, many of the places I passed days ago, buzz by, barely visible behind the glass. And yet each of them vivid in mind: the university proud on the hill, the whirling city square where I met the bored tailor and stood before the statue, the Hollow Man, and the quiet, forlorn library.

Each place slips by as if it's an unfinished story. It's strange. I thought I'd been stuck in this town. Now it feels like it's slipping past me, some final procession of all its quiet unraveling.

Silence reigns in the car. After what passed between the driver and me, unsayable and unspeaking, words would fall like clatter, awkward and flat. The driver doesn't say, but I can feel it—this route isn't random. He's retracing something. Mapping my steps. Framing it all.

It's ironic, in a town blurred and darkened by plague, the

clarity by which I see it now, God in the acid bath. The town tried to build something without him. A new kind of religion, modern and human. But it couldn't carry the weight and devastation, not of this insufferable plague.

It reminds me of Lake Superior. Its steely gray depths. The way the water can sit quietly, pretending peace, while beneath, it keeps the wreckage of lives who underestimated what it can hold.

That's Novemberton. An abyss of black cloud, a foreboding riddle.

We pass the corner near the café, where it all began, and where I first gazed at the woman scrolling. I wonder about her now, what became of her on that fateful afternoon when she disappeared into the crowd.

We stop. St. Bartholomew's.

The church is smaller than I remember. Moss, damp and thick, spreads across its walkway. The ash-gray granite shows only the slow persistence of weather. I climb the steps. The old bulletin board still hangs beside the door. I hadn't noticed the cracks in the glass last time. Tiny fractures, spidering out from the corner. It hasn't changed much, but standing here again, I realize that I have.

The driver keeps his hands on the wheel. His voice, when it comes, is low. "These bells don't toll no more," he says. "Stopped a long time ago."

He doesn't wait for a response, doesn't turn. Just drives off, leaving the moment open. I stand for a moment, watching the taillights disappear into the morning haze.

Then I turn back to the church.

ATHEISM TO ASHES

In 2025, columnist Giles Coren wrote a piece for *The Times* at the start of Lent, titled "This Lent I Will Turn Atheism to Ashes." A self-described "lapsed atheist," Coren recounts how his decision to give up atheism began one Ash Wednesday, when a vicar dipped his finger into palm ash, marked Coren's forehead with a cross, and reminded him, "You are dust, and to dust you shall return."

In the piece, Coren argues that atheism has become the default stance of modern adulthood. It arrives with birth certificates, embedded in a culture shaped by nihilism. Science, reason, and the relentless flood of information deepen its hold, making unbelief seem inevitable. Yet, he notes, atheists often fail to see how fully saturated society already is with their worldview. "Many atheists think we want to hear their irrefutable arguments against belief and witty put-downs of the faithful," he writes, "but I just wonder, 'Why do you bother? To whom are you talking? Who do you think is not already an atheist?'" He sees the world as a kind of Novemberton.

Still, his experience with atheism, he admits, "left a hole."

"My childhood was godless," he writes, "and there was room for improvement."

The death of his father was a turning point. "It seemed to me, at the very end, that God might have been useful to him [his father]. And it would certainly have helped us, when we buried him, to have had some formal tradition for the ceremony, rather than having to make it up as we went along."

It was his son who eventually led him back.

One day, the boy, raised like him, in no tradition at all, said he wanted to go to church.

"I said okay . . . And we've been going ever since."

In that small parish, Coren found what atheism could not offer: substance, beauty, and enchantment.

"Inside, it is vast, awesomely rectilinear and full of light from the high windows that are gently stained but only in squares, not pictures . . . The congregation is small but intense . . . The homily is always good, the organ music magical. There are bells and incense, bowing and genuflecting, a snug Eucharist and much talk of saints and the Virgin . . . And I have a sense that God is there—in the tradition, the words, the two thousand years of conviction, the imagination of all the people who came before me."[1]

He ends with a memory: his grandfather's burial, beside a muddy hole in a bleak cemetery. His father, who had long abandoned faith, stood by the grave, weeping. Coren longed for something more than a surrender to that kind of despair.

BARTH'S ISSUE WITH REASON

Coren, in abandoning atheism, acknowledges the limits of human reason. In doing so, he implies that certain aspects of human experience lie beyond its reach. His experience illustrates the view of Karl Barth, the Swiss Reformed theologian widely regarded as the most influential Christian thinker of the twentieth century. Barth's *Church Dogmatics*, his monumental theological work, centers on the idea that God revealed himself to the world through Christ.

In Barth's era, Europe, like Novemberton, had come of age. Faith, once assumed, now had to justify itself before the tribunal of Enlightenment reason. Theologians scrambled to reconcile mystery with modernity, seeking to bridge belief with the demands of science and human autonomy.

Barth was troubled by this. He saw it as a compromise, an attempt to play by modernism's rules without acknowledging the limits of those rules. For him, human beings cannot grasp God through rationalist frameworks. Divine revelation is something given, not deduced.

Nietzsche might have felt that Barth's concept of God lacked grounding in reality, that revelation without reason is delusion. But Barth could respond by challenging that very premise. Human reasoning, he claimed, is inherently limited. There is an insurmountable gap between God and man, and reason cannot bridge it. The absence of answers to every metaphysical question, Barth insisted, is not a reason to reject God. Faith, for him, means trusting the revelation we've been given, even when it cannot be fully grasped. He called this "the hiddenness of God": the truth that God is not a thing among other things, not a concept we can hold or dissect.

He wrote, "The assertion of God's hiddenness (which includes God's invisibility, incomprehensibility, and ineffability) tells us that God does not belong to the objects which we can always subjugate to the process of our viewing, conceiving, and expressing, and therefore our spiritual oversight and control. In contrast to that of all other objects, his nature is not one which in this sense lies in the sphere of our power. God is inapprehensible."[2]

God's hiddenness, then, reflects not his insufficiency but ours. Attempting to know him on our own terms, Barth warned, leads to shipwreck, the collapse of self-sufficiency. That collapse appears in figures like Coren, whose existential ache reveals the failure of reason to bear ultimate meaning, especially in moments of suffering, plague, or death.

> It is because the fellowship between God and us is established and continues by God's grace that God is hidden from us. All of our efforts to apprehend him by ourselves shipwreck on this. He is always the one who will first and foremost apprehend and possess us. It is only on the basis of this, and in the area marked out by it, that there can and should be our own apprehension of God.[3]

Barth might argue that modernity's "murder" of God is proof not of his absence but of our hubris, our refusal to accept the limits of our understanding. The belief that reason can fully grasp the divine, the soul, or the mystery of suffering, what Barth might call the Mood of Reason, was a doomed path from the beginning. It led not to freedom but to nihilism.

Against this, Barth stood firm. His theology refused to reduce God to a system. He subordinated reason to divine revelation and invited faith to wager not on certainty but on trust.

Coren's return to church, despite years of disbelief, reflects this same shift. Like the columnist, he steps into a space that points beyond the intellect—something higher, something mysterious. He surrenders to the possibility that God cannot be grasped through analysis. As he puts it, simply, "We're all just ash, aren't we?"

Barth, Coren, and the columnist all agree. Reason and philosophy may take us far, but not far enough. If we are to find something eternal, healing, and reconciling, it must come not from within us but from beyond.

ARTLESS

The recent visits to the church, despite the absence of formal services, reveal something deeper about Novemberton. What does it say about the townspeople's confidence in a godless world if they still cross the threshold of a sanctuary not to believe but simply to sit?

The ways they've tried to bear nihilism have proven too fragile. The burden is too immense. The church, by contrast, doesn't make demands. It doesn't require assent. It simply remains a silent witness to the collapse of all the systems that tried to replace it. And somehow that's enough to draw them in.

They come in quietly. Sit in the pews. Stare at dust drifting through the dim air, suspended like memory. Some speak. Most don't. The church doesn't answer their questions. It just holds them, offering a shoulder broad enough for the kind of despair modernity refuses to see, the sorrow reason cannot soothe. A silence not vacant but veiled. And in refusing to explain itself, it becomes sacred.

In its stillness, the church stands as a quiet critique of godless Novemberton, a world where faith has been traded for screens, silence drowned beneath the noise of zettabytes and curated distraction. The more the town has filled itself with the excess of information, the emptier it seems to have become.

And in that vacuum, the church remains, not with answers but with presence.

It echoes Barth's assertion that atheism is "an artless and childish"[4] form of religion: "It [atheism] denies the existence of God and the validity of divine law. And its whole interest is the denial of such. This is artless. It fails to see what mysticism does not fail to see—that absolute denial can have no meaning . . . Atheism lives in and by its negation. It can only break down and take away, and therefore it is exposed to the constant danger of finishing at a dead end."[5]

Barth argued that faith and divine revelation possess a mystique that reason alone cannot reach. They compel humanity not to solve but to pause, to look again. Art, in particular, embodies this mystical essence. It doesn't persuade by logic. It draws us in by beauty. It engages what lies beyond utility, whispering truths that transcend comprehension.

For Barth, atheism denies the essence of humanity, stifling the faculties that nurture creativity and depth. It is the narrowing of human life to only what can be measured or explained. It denies the very faculties that allow us to create meaning.

Relying solely on reason to understand life reduces it to a cycle of endless, shrinking questions. Like a child who won't stop asking, "Why?"

Why is it bedtime?

Because it's late.

Why is it late?

Because the earth rotates.

Why does the earth rotate?

Because it does.

Why?

Eventually, you run out of answers. You exhaust the thread. But that's not where the night ends. When the little scientist finally settles, you tell them a bedtime story about a castle, a dragon, a hero. Something enchanting, beautiful, and true in a way facts can't be. Reminding them that some truths lie beyond reason, in the realm of imagination and wonder.

Maybe it's just me, but I've always admired children for that. They don't segment their minds. They don't apologize for wanting to be moved. They don't demand that the world be provable before it can be meaningful. They trust what stirs them. They honor their whole selves.

Maybe we're the ones who've forgotten how to marvel. Barth never saw imagination as an escape. He saw it as a way of knowing, a way of receiving what the intellect alone cannot hold.

Theologian Makoto Fujimura emphasizes this: "Because the God of the Bible is fundamentally and exclusively *the* Creator, God cannot be known by talking about God, or by debating God's existence (even if we 'win' the debate). God cannot be known by sitting in a classroom . . . God the Artist communicates to us first, before God the lecturer."[6]

Ellen Davis echoes it: "It is through our imagination that God reaches us." She's not talking about fantasy or delusion. Rather she refers to "the mental and spiritual capacities that the biblical writers call the 'heart' . . . the organ that alerts us to what God is doing in our lives or the world."[7]

Fujimura calls art the "perfect vehicle" for divine knowledge because it speaks to all the senses, senses Barth believed modernity had dulled. These are the same senses that stir in Novemberton's people when they enter the sanctuary. They don't believe, not fully. But they feel. Something in them remembers or wants to.

And the church?

It doesn't explain. It just stands there.

Quietly insisting there's more.

WHAT TO IMAGINE

In 1971, John Lennon wrote "Imagine." Lennon was, to put it mildly, an artist. Beyond his groundbreaking work with the Beatles, he sketched and scribbled surreal, dreamlike pieces, fragments that mirrored the spirit of his music. His art, like his politics, was built on imagining a world set free.

He once said, "If art were to redeem man, it could do so only by saving him from the seriousness of life and restoring him to an unexpected boyishness."[8] It was a playful critique of rationality, a belief that reason alone is too thin a beam to carry the weight of real life.

Lennon was deeply disturbed by the Vietnam War. Agent Orange, body counts, trauma, draft cards. And he blamed religion. The structure of it. The violence done in its name. So he wrote a song and used his lyrics to invite listeners to imagine a world without heaven, hell, nations, or even religion. Only sky. Only each other.

As a kid, I first caught this song on New Year's Eve, blaring from the TV while the crowds in Times Square eagerly counted down to midnight, welcoming yet another year. There they were, swaying back and forth, singing along to Lennon's euphoric melody, imagining all the endless possibilities of the coming year.

I admired that he was willing to imagine.

But what if the substance of that imagination was wrong?

I once played golf in California with a couple who brought it up, unprompted. By the sixth hole, the conversation had drifted to religion.

They chimed, "Our son's in college. He hates his religion classes. All of them. And honestly, we don't blame him. Religion is the problem."

It's a familiar response. Like Lennon, like many others, they see religion as the weight, not the lift.

And so came Novemberton, this strange place where that very idea has been tested to its limits. The place I imagined. The town I am walking through. A world without God, without certainty, with only truths we carry, but none that carry us.

A world without religion. No transcendence. No tradition. No sacred story.

Only screens, slogans, systems, and selves.

And it plays out like a warning:

1. *Progress Without Purpose*: advancing in technology but with no lasting why.
2. *Boredom and Hollowness*: a quiet desperation masked by memes and distractions.
3. *Existential Emptiness*: the constant hum that nothing truly matters.
4. *The Fall of the Man-God*: self-exaltation collapsing under its own weight.
5. *Surrender to the Plague*: no reason, no redemptive arc, just suffering.
6. *No Escape*: every path to meaning ends in futility: activism, irony, consumption.

So was Lennon right?

It's true he was willing to imagine. That takes courage—believe me, I know. But the world he asked us to picture, a world stripped of religion and wonder, may not be the better world he had hoped for.

And in this world that I've created, the townspeople are starting to feel it too.

They don't just pass the church. They step inside. They sit. They breathe in the silence. Maybe, without quite knowing why, they're beginning to imagine again not the absence of heaven but the possibility of something higher. Not just sky above us but a presence that holds the world together.

Maybe that's why they keep returning.

To imagine something larger than themselves.

IN ST. BARTHOLOMEW'S

I press the door open. I hadn't noticed the scent of wood before, its warm amber sweetness not dulled by years of use. I walk in, and on the far wall I see a crucifix. The Savior hangs there, arms outstretched, head bowed, draped in webs and dust so thick it softens even the wounds.

Two doors lead into the sanctuary. This time, I choose the one on the left.

Rows of wooden pews stretch out before the altar. I notice now, more clearly, that each window depicts a biblical story, disciples and saints. I imagine how they must have looked once, vibrant colors cast across their faces, light moving through them. Now they stand steeped in shadow.

I make my way toward the front. On the pew behind mine, a hymnal lies open, pages curled, softened by the decay of many years. The scent of paper drifts up—faint, but full. Worn in from having been held often by many hands.

I sit down and reach for it. The cover flakes slightly beneath my hand. The spine stays open naturally, as though that person had left it this way, a page worn down by touch and time.

And then I see the words.

Silent night, holy night
All is calm, all is bright
Round yon virgin, mother and child
Holy infant so tender and mild
Sleep in heavenly peace
Sleep in heavenly peace

Silent night, holy night
Shepherds quake at the sight
Glories stream from heaven afar
Heavenly hosts sing Alleluia
Christ the Savior is born
Christ the Savior is born

Silent night, holy night
Son of God, love's pure light
Radiant beams from thy holy face
With the dawn of redeeming grace

Jesus, Lord, at thy birth
Jesus, Lord, at thy birth

The dust dims the ink but not the meaning. A fragment of beauty preserved in the darkness of winter.

I wonder who sat here before me, what they were hoping to remember or forget. I wonder whether something in these lyrics stirred them, the virgin with child, the glories streaming from heaven, the light on the face of a savior.

After my journey, this hymnal doesn't feel ordinary. In a town that tried to kill God with reason, it feels instead like a book of wonder, a bridge to something sacred, tucked between paper and page. A reminder that, even now, something beyond the mind still stirs the heart.

IMAGINE: IMMANUEL, GOD WITH US

Karl Barth offered a striking perspective on atheism. He didn't just challenge it, he denied its possibility. No matter how fiercely we try to construct a world without God, Barth believed such efforts always fail. Divine revelation, he argued, cannot be undone by human autonomy. God has chosen to be with humankind. And nothing, not even our forgetting, can undo that choice.

Man can be godless. But God does not become manless. He is always the creator and lord of man. And because he is not "manless," the godlessness of man can only be a human notion. Man "cannot really escape God. His godlessness may be very strong, but it cannot make God a manless God."[9]

So even if Novemberton feels hollow, with its depraved panelists, its thinkers drowning in information, its desperate grasp for meaning and purpose, God remains mysteriously present.

Barth saw God's nearness not in triumph but in mercy: in that even after our rebellion has run its course, even when nihilism has stripped the soul bare, God still abides. "It is a divine mercy that atheism cannot provide a final word about itself . . . for while humanity may choose to live without God, God has elected from eternity to live with and for humanity."[10]

Sitting in the pew, as the final notes of "Silent Night" fade, I look again at the stained glass, at a child in a manger, wrapped in cloth, surrounded by animals, shepherds, and two weary parents.

For a moment, I close my eyes. And then a warmth I haven't felt since I arrived here begins to rise in me. I open them. Light filters through the glass and wraps its long limbs of reds, blues, and golds around the manger, spilling out across the sanctuary floor, reaching for me.

Has he been here all along?

In the pub.

In the scrolling silence of the woman at the café.

In the IT guy's cramped office.

At the hospital, when the child clutched his teddy.

Was he there?

Was this town ever truly free of him?

The answer doesn't come in logic.

It arrives in color.

In this beauty set before me.

In light.

ENTERING LIGHT

To cite the most brilliant of thinkers, there's an old song Relient K once wrote about winter, "In Like a Lion (Always Winter)," not just about the season but about the feeling. That long ache of waiting. They called it always winter, never Christmas. A frozen loop of meaninglessness. A curse without a counterspell.

They imagined something more. The winter lifting, the cold skies breaking, hearts warmed not by explanation but by expectation. The promise of green grass on the other side. A sigh beside the fire. A flicker of hope that survives the frost.

They imagined the incarnation as a silent night that floods the deepest parts of the human soul with its creator. In this, there is hope that winter can be endured for the promise of Christmas, an event that gave meaning to humanity's despair. Unlike Lennon, they saw God not as the problem but as the answer.

A light that doesn't explain away the darkness but enters it.

Sitting here now, I realize that's what pulled me into the hospital chapel that night. Not proof. Not resolve. But faith in someone solid. Someone tender. Someone real enough to hold me up.

On that dismal night, I sat there because there was nowhere else to go. And when I looked up, I saw it, the nativity on the wall. Maybe I didn't know it then, but it was that very hope, the hope of Christmas, that had drawn me in from the cold and into that little chapel.

Nothing else could hold the weight of what I carried. Not the degrees. Not the success. Not the house, the books, the curated life. Not even the strength I'd always leaned on in myself.

Nothing had been strong enough to shoulder the weight of my mother's ill-timed illness. And for once, I had no answers, just an ache too deep for words.

Sitting down in that smallness was its own kind of surrender, a letting go of will, of intellect, of explanation. It wasn't reason that brought me there but exhaustion. Desperation.

And in that stillness, the image remained, stirring something in me.

It wasn't a doctrine. It wasn't even comfort. It was beauty, the kind that doesn't argue, only stretches out its arms.

The painting illuminated a truth I'd known but forgotten: "'The virgin will conceive and give birth to a son, and they will call him Immanuel' (which means 'God with us')" (Matt. 1:23).

There, in the face of disease and death, I saw something that couldn't be reasoned into being. Art had done what philosophy couldn't. It had revealed. And what it revealed was this: The virgin would conceive. The child would come. And he would be called Immanuel. God with us.

And now, in this town that I've created, this shadow of the world I've walked through, I begin to see how that same image might be calling others back. The townspeople who sit quietly in the church. The ones who don't speak. Who don't quite believe. Who don't yet hope.

But they imagine.

And that's how it begins.

It gives them, and gave me, a promise: that in the middle of winter, they can still have Christmas. Not as sentiment but as defiance. A holy wager against the cold. And Christmas, the celebration of the incarnation, becomes something more than memory. It becomes the moment when God, once buried in abstraction, rises from the acid bath not in triumph but in tenderness. Not to shame the thinkers but to touch the grieving.

To hold the child.

To speak into the silence that reason cannot fill.

This is the answer to the ghost at the feast, the one who haunted every lecture, every panel discussion, every quiet moment in this town. The one who whispered, "There is nothing more."

And perhaps that ghost will always haunt our reason. But he cannot touch what lives deeper, the imagination that aches for God, even when it cannot name him.

The longing that outlasts despair.

The kind of hope that does not need to explain itself to exist.

HOPE FOR NOVEMBERTON

Millennia ago, Ambrose of Milan (c. AD 340–397) believed that God did not choose to save the world through reason. The intellect, he argued, cannot lift humanity out of the darkness of its soul. His view ran against the prevailing mood of his time, and ours, which assumed reason governs all. But Ambrose insisted it never had. Reason does not rule the passions. Nor will it, no matter how far we evolve.

In that same spirit, James K. A. Smith calls for a shift from reason to imagination in our search for meaning. He calls it "conquering from the imagination up." He writes, "The logician speaks a tongue foreign to the heart. Poetry, literature, and painting are a glossolalia that the imagination hears in its own language. And in imagining, we may learn how to be human again."[11]

Imagination makes the Christmas story possible. And more than that, it makes human life possible. To imagine something that gives us hope is not a luxury. It's a necessity. We not only *should* do it, we must. Our nature calls us to it.

I saw this during the COVID pandemic.

The strangest thing about that spring wasn't the silence or even the fear. It was the carols. Everywhere. "Silent Night," "Joy to the World," not tucked behind December but echoing through March and April. I made a playlist to keep the panic out. My brother, an ER nurse, said the ICU staff sang quietly while tending the sick. A friend even hung Christmas lights in their living room.

It was as if, at the end of reason, we reached for wonder. In the chaos, there was something deeply human—and deeply right—about imagining a savior in a manger. It was conquering from the imagination.

As I sit in a pew, hymnal still open, the words of "Silent Night" still lingering in the air and the image of the incarnation glowing in the stained glass, something deeper than thought is awakened.

Novemberton was born when reason was exalted above all, and everything else was dissolved. But we are more than logic. We are creatures who ache for meaning, for what heals and reconciles. And we do ourselves no favors by silencing the part of us that still believes a savior has come. Not to explain or expound but to redeem.

The preacher once said, "For with much wisdom comes

much sorrow; the more knowledge, the more grief" (Eccl. 1:18), and Novemberton bears it out. But it is cruel to silence the parts of ourselves that long to imagine that a child was born and that his coming can answer the suffering.

As I sit before the painting of the virgin birth, now resplendent in light, it hits me. The warmth I feel is sunlight. For the first time, it has broken into this plague-ridden town.

I step out into the cold, but its bite no longer gnaws at me. The streets look the same, yet something has shifted. A quiet hope walks beside me.

A few steps on, I pause and turn back.

The church door sways gently, and I realize someone else has just entered.

It seems the columnist was right. He isn't the only one willing to imagine, to wager, to wonder, to rise from the acid bath and answer the ghost not with theory but with presence.

Almost as if he knew it, the taxi driver rounds the corner. He doesn't speak as I climb in, but something in him is different. His eyes, clear now, shine as if the tears have begun to wash away his fear.

We pull forward.

Then, a sound. Low, resonant, it echoes through the foggy streets in a summons long forgotten but now remembered.

He gestures to the display on the dash.

And there it is.

A single date.

Simple. Unassuming. But this time, it feels like more than a date.

A crack in the gray.

A line in the sky.

Hope for this cold little town.

December 1.

ACKNOWLEDGMENTS

This is the book I've always wanted to write: an imaginative exploration of philosophy, theology, and the search for meaning. I wrote it in an empty house with no furniture, often in the early hours of the morning. It would have been easy to feel alone in the process, but I wasn't.

I want to thank those who have been with me in this journey:

Whitney Gossett, you were the first to believe in this book. I remember telling you about it in Austin, over sushi, while feeling like I was rambling. You supported me and helped turn those ramblings into reality.

Kandace McCorister and Jayne Lee, or as our group text calls you, The Book Squad: Your expertise gave me the confidence to keep going, knowing I had the support it takes to write a book like this. You both are brilliant.

My CORE 3113 class at Southeastern University: Developing this book with you was a blast. I'll never forget the lecture on the delivery driver. I doubt I'll ever laugh as much in a lecture setting again.

The staff and faculty at the Barnett College of Ministry and Theology at Southeastern University: Thank you for listening to my ideas, offering wisdom, and sharing in the humor of the process.

Zondervan: Your collaboration from start to finish has been exceptional.

And finally, my family.

NOTES

Chapter 1: November of the Soul

1. Alan Watts, "The Tao of Philosophy 1," The Library of Consciousness, accessed April 19, 2025, www.organism.earth/library/document/tao-of-philosophy-1.
2. David Gerrold, *Alternate Gerrolds: An Assortment of Fictitious Lives* (Dallas: BenBella Books, 2004), 201.
3. Emil Cioran, *The Trouble with Being Born*, trans. Richard Howard (New York: Arcade, 1973), 14.
4. William Shakespeare, *Macbeth*, ed. Stephen Orgel (New York: Penguin, 2016), 92.
5. Dietrich Bonhoeffer, *Letters and Papers from Prison*, ed. Eberhard Bethge (New York: Simon and Schuster, 2011), 340.
6. u/thinkpiecefactory, "Analysis of 'All Eyes on Me,'" *Reddit*, r/boburnham, May 31, 2021, www.reddit.com/r/boburnham/comments/npcazu/analysis_of_all_eyes_on_me/.
7. Since 2023, the total private student-loan debt has increased by 11.1 percent. The average monthly payment among student-loan holders is between $200 and $299. University graduates owe an average of $28,244 after they leave school. See Melanie Hanson, "Average Student Loan Debt [2024]," Education Data Initiative, last updated August 16, 2024, https://educationdata.org/average-student-loan-debt.
8. Housing affordability is determined using the ratio of house prices to wages. The ratio indicates how many years of salary it would take to buy a home. In the 1960s, the ratio was

4.4 years, meaning it would take 4.4 years of the average annual wage to buy a home. As of 2024, the ratio is 7.6 years. Despite growth in annual wage, buying a home continues to become increasingly difficult. It's not the fraps, Mom and Dad! See Roger Wood, "US House Price vs Average Annual Salary: 1963–2024," TimeTrex, July 11, 2024, www.timetrex.com /blog/us-house-prices-vs-wages.

9. E-cigarette sales, as well as e-cigarette brands, increased by more than 46 percent between January 2020 and December 2022. Disposable e-cigarettes nearly tripled in nicotine strength, quintupled in capacity, and dropped in price by 70 percent between 2017 and 2022. See Truth Initiative, "E-Cigarettes: Facts, Stats and Regulations," October 16, 2024, https://truthinitiative.org/research-resources/emerging -tobacco-products/e-cigarettes-facts-stats-and-regulations.
10. Overall sales of nicotine pouches in the United States went from 126.06 million units in 2019 to 808.14 million units in March 2022. Sales products with 8 mg nicotine-concentration levels increased more rapidly than products with lower concentration levels. See Anuja Majmundar et al., "Nicotine Pouch Sales Trends in the US by Volume and Nicotine Concentration Levels from 2019 to 2022," *JAMA Network Open* 5, no. 11 (November 15, 2022): e2242235, doi:10.1001 /jamanetworkopen.2022.42235.
11. In July 2024, *Forbes* reported that the S&P 500 Textiles Apparel and Luxury Goods Industry Index had slumped almost 30 percent, with brands like Hugo Boss and Burberry seeing significant sales drops in Asia and the Americas. See Alicia Park, "Luxury Fashion Is Struggling in the First Half of 2024—Here's Why," *Forbes*, July 17, 2024, updated July 23, 2024, www.forbes.com/sites/aliciapark/2024/07/17/designer -fashion-houses-are-struggling-in-the-first-half-of-2024-heres -why/.
12. Porn makes up 12 percent of the internet, and the most popular pornographic website receives 42 billion visits per year. See Jessica Miller, "Porn Addiction Statistics," *AddictionHelp*

.com, last updated July 30, 2025, www.addictionhelp.com/porn/statistics/.

13. In October 2024, an adult content creator made international headlines by sleeping with 101 men in fourteen hours. The event became part of a documentary in which she described the experience as "robotic." See Claudia Poposki, "Sex Worker Who Slept with 639 People in 2024 Weighs In on OnlyFans Model Lily Phillips' '100 Men' Challenge," *New York Post*, December 21, 2024, https://nypost.com/2024/12/21/lifestyle/sex-worker-who-slept-with-639-people-in-2024-weighs-in-on-lily-phillips-100-men-challenge/.
14. Research between the Section of Urology at the University of Chicago Medicine and the UChicago Center for Health and Social Sciences points to a growing number of vasectomies. Findings revealed that the percentage of male patients undergoing vasectomies in a given year increased from .427 percent in 2014 to .537 percent in 2021. Though this number is only 4 percent of men being sterilized, it does suggest changing values, as medical professionals believe the number will continue to grow. See Grace Niewijk, "Insurance Data Reveal That Vasectomies Are Becoming More Common in the U.S.," UChicago Medicine, August 21, 2023, www.uchicagomedicine.org/forefront/surgery-articles/vasectomy-trends-research.
15. As of 2021, 25 percent of forty-year-olds in the United States had never been married. This was an increase from 20 percent in 2010. See Richard Fry, "A Record-High Share of 40-Year-Olds in the U.S. Have Never Been Married," *Pew Research Center*, June 28, 2023, www.pewresearch.org/short-reads/2023/06/28/a-record-high-share-of-40-year-olds-in-the-us-have-never-been-married/. Sex researcher Dr. Amy Moors found in a study that the number of people in the United States who would like to engage in a polyamorous relationship is one in six. Don't think that's a lot? That is about the same as the number of people who own a cat. See Kinsey Institute, "Polyamory and Consensual Non-monogamy

in the US," Kinsey Institute Blog, June 17, 2022, https://blogs.iu.edu/kinseyinstitute/2022/06/17/polyamory-and-consensual-non-monogamy-in-the-us/.

16. A whopping 84 percent of millennials and Gen Z say they've been ghosted. While this causes confusion and sadness, three in four people think ghosting is acceptable at times and almost two in three people have ghosted someone else. See "Report: Top Six Reasons Gen Z and Millennials Ghost," Thriving Center of Psychology, September 21, 2023, https://thrivingcenterofpsych.com/blog/gen-z-millennial-ghosting-statistics/.
17. Almost 50 percent of people in 2024 said they were considering quitting their jobs. See Morgan Smith, "Nearly 50% of People Are Considering Leaving Their Jobs in 2024—More Than During the 'Great Resignation,'" CNBC, May 8, 2024, www.cnbc.com/2024/05/08/nearly-50percent-of-people-are-considering-leaving-their-jobs-in-2024.html. While there are various reasons for this, among Gen Z in particular, the main is that their jobs are not fulfilling. Seventy-two percent of Gen Zers surveyed said that having a satisfying job is more important than salary. See Tracy Brower, "Gen Zs Are Quitting in Droves: Six Best Ways to Retain Them," *Forbes*, September 24, 2023, www.forbes.com/sites/tracybrower/2023/09/24/gen-zs-are-quitting-in-droves-6-best-ways-to-retain-them/.
18. In a 2023 survey, Customer Contact Week Digital found that 57 percent of customers surveyed believed that customer service had gotten worse in the last year, with a quarter of all those surveyed saying it had become much worse. See Roger Dooley, "Is Customer Experience in Decline?" *Forbes*, June 30, 2023, www.forbes.com/sites/rogerdooley/2023/06/30/is-customer-experience-in-decline/.
19. Only 21 percent of Americans attend a religious service every week. Fifty-six percent say they seldom attend and 31 percent say they never attend. Just two decades ago, an average of 42 percent of US adults attended a religious service every

week or nearly every week. Most religious groups have seen a decline in regular attendance at religious services over the past two decades. See Jeffrey M. Jones, "Church Attendance Has Declined in Most U.S. Religious Groups," Gallup, March 25, 2024, news.gallup.com/poll/642548/church-attendance-declined-religious-groups.aspx.

20. See Ecclesiastes 2.
21. Matthew Arnold, "Dover Beach," in *The Oxford Book of English Verse*, ed. Christopher Ricks (Oxford: Clarendon, 1999), 453–54.

Chapter 2: God in the Acid Bath

1. Friedrich Nietzsche, *The Joyous Science*, trans. R. Kevin Hill (New York: Penguin, 2018), 133–34.
2. For a thorough analysis of the various ages of Western religiousness, see James C. Edwards, *The Plain Sense of Things* (University Park, PA: Pennsylvania University Press, 1997), 1–57.
3. Tremper Longman III, *The Book of Ecclesiastes* (Grand Rapids: Eerdmans, 1998), 282.
4. *The Epic of Gilgamesh*, trans. N. K. Sanders (New York: Penguin, 1972), 43.
5. Homer, *The Odyssey*, trans. Robert Fagles (New York: Penguin, 1997), 504–5.
6. Plato, *The Republic* (Global Publishers, 2024), 251, Kindle.
7. René Descartes, *Meditations of First Philosophy*, 2nd ed., trans. John Cottingham (Cambridge: Cambridge University Press, 2017), 20.
8. Descartes, *Meditations*, 22.
9. Edwards, *Plain Sense of Things*, 29.
10. Friedrich Nietzsche, *Beyond Good and Evil*, trans. R. J. Hollingdale (New York: Penguin, 2003), 23–24.
11. Friedrich Nietzsche, *The Will to Power*, trans. R. Kevin Hill and Michael A. Scarpitti (New York: Penguin, 2017), 595–96.
12. Nietzsche, *Will to Power*, 33.

Chapter 3: The Ghost at the Feast

1. T. S. Eliot, "The Hollow Men," Poetry Foundation, accessed April 19, 2025, https://poets.org/poem/hollow-men.
2. William Shakespeare, *Macbeth*, ed. Stephen Orgel (New York: Penguin, 2016), 53–54.
3. See Friedrich Nietzsche, *The Will to Power*, trans. R. Kevin Hill and Michael A. Scarpitti (New York: Penguin, 2017), 38, for Nietzsche's understanding of active and passive nihilism.
4. See David Foster Wallace, *This Is Water* (New York: Little, Brown, 2009), 77, 84.
5. *Humanist Manifestos I and II*, ed. Paul Kurtz (Essex, CT: Prometheus, 1973), 16.
6. Kurtz, *Humanist Manifestos I and II*, 17.
7. See Baron Paul Henri Thiry d'Holbach, *Good Sense* (Library of Alexandria, 2009).

Chapter 4: Rise of the Monsters and Trolls

1. Neil Postman, *Amusing Ourselves to Death: Public Discourse in the Age of Show Business* (New York: Penguin, 2005), xxi.
2. David Bawden and Lyn Robinson, "The Dark Side of Information: Overload, Anxiety, and Other Paradoxes and Pathologies," *Journal of Information Science* 35, no. 2 (2009): 180–91.
3. Statista, "Data Growth Worldwide 2010–2028," accessed February 21, 2025, www.statista.com/statistics/871513/world wide-data-created/.
4. Albert Camus, *Carnets 1942–51*, trans. Philip Thody (London: Hamish Hamilton, 1966), 9, quoted in Matthew Sharpe, "The Black Side of the Sun: Camus, Theology, and the Problem of Evil," *Political Theology* 15, no. 2 (2014): 151–74.
5. Matt Pocius on Tesla Stock and Money, "Elon Musk's NEW EPIC Rant!" YouTube, June 16, 2021, www.youtube.com /watch?v=dRZUt6tu8bw.
6. Mary Shelley, *Frankenstein* (New York: Penguin, 2018), 39.
7. Shelley, *Frankenstein*, 54.

8. Søren Kierkegaard, *Søren Kierkegaards Papirer* VII A 540, 1848, in *Journals and Papers*, ed. and trans. Howard V. Hong and Edna H. Hong, vol. 2 (Bloomington: Indiana University Press, 1970), entry 2152.
9. Søren Kierkegaard, *The Present Age: On the Death of Rebellion*, trans. Alesander Dru (New York: HarperPerennial, 1962), 61.

Chapter 5: Dark Catechism

1. Fyodor Dostoyevsky, *Demons*, trans. Ronald Meyer and Robert Maguire (New York: Penguin Classics, 2008), 682.
2. Dostoyevsky, *Demons*, 682.
3. Dostoyevsky, *Demons*, 127–28.
4. Dostoyevsky, *Demons*, 264.
5. Dostoyevsky, *Demons*, 745.
6. Dostoyevsky, *Demons*, 745.
7. Fyodor Dostoyevsky, *The Brothers Karamazov*, trans. Richard Pevear and Larissa Volokhonsky (New York: Picador, 2002), 259–60.
8. Dostoyevsky, *Brothers Karamazov*, 260.
9. Dostoyevsky, *Brothers Karamazov*, 688.
10. Fyodor Dostoyevsky, *Crime and Punishment*, trans. David McDuff (New York: Penguin, 2003), 308.
11. Dostoyevsky, *Crime and Punishment*, 79.
12. Carl Sagan, *Cosmos* (New York: Ballantine, 2013), 1.
13. *Humanist Manifestos I and II*, ed. Paul Kurtz (Essex, CT: Prometheus, 1973), 17.

Chapter 6: Stuck In Self-Destruct

1. Fyodor Dostoyevsky, *Notes from Underground and the Double*, trans. Ronald Wilks (New York: Penguin, 2009), 3.
2. Dostoyevsky, *Notes*, 28.
3. Dostoyevsky, *Notes*, 44.
4. Dostoyevsky, *Notes*, 46.
5. Dostoyevsky, *Notes*, 46–47.

6. Dostoyevsky, *Notes*, 50.
7. Dostoyevsky, *Notes*, 57.
8. Dostoyevsky, *Notes*, 61.
9. Dostoyevsky, *Notes*, 69.
10. Dostoyevsky, *Notes*, 78.
11. Dostoyevsky, *Notes*, 89.
12. Dostoyevsky, *Notes*, 92.
13. Dostoyevsky, *Notes*, 96.
14. Dostoyevsky, *Notes*, 111.
15. Dostoyevsky, *Notes*, 113.
16. Dostoyevsky, *Notes*, 118.
17. Eduard Thurneysen, *Dostoyevsky*, trans. Keith Crim (Eugene, OR: Wipf and Stock, 1964), 14.

Chapter 7: The Plague Settles In

1. Albert Camus, *The Plague*, trans. Stuart Gilbert (New York: Random House, 1991), 223.
2. Camus, *Plague*, 37.
3. Camus, *Plague*, 37.
4. Thomas Nagel, "The Absurd," *Journal of Philosophy* 68, no. 20 (1971): 717.
5. Albert Camus, *Carnets 1941–1951*, trans. Philip Thody (London: Hamish Hamilton, 1966), 9, 52.
6. Albert Camus, *The Rebel: An Essay on Man in Revolt*, trans. Anthony Bower (New York: Vintage, 1992), 35.
7. Camus, *Rebel*, 26.
8. Camus, *Rebel*, 101–2.

Chapter 8: Acting Our Way Out

1. Os Guinness, *The Case for Civility: And Why Our Future Depends on It* (San Francisco: HarperOne, 2009), 15.
2. Albert Camus, *The Stranger*, trans. Matthew Ward (New York: Vintage, 1989), 3.
3. Camus, *Stranger*, 58–59.
4. Camus, *Stranger*, 58.

Chapter 9: Laughing Our Way Out

1. Adult Swim, "Roy: A Life Well Lived | Rick and Morty | Adult Swim," YouTube video, August 30, 2016, www.youtube.com/watch?v=szzVlQ653as.

Chapter 10: Indulging Our Way Out

1. William Ernest Henley, "Invictus," Poetry Foundation, accessed April 22, 2025, www.poetryfoundation.org/poems/51642/invictus.
2. Jean Paul Sartre, *Nausea*, trans. Lloyd Alexander (New York: New Directions, 2007), 126–27.

Chapter 11: A Wager on Transcendence

1. Jean Paul, *Flower, Fruit, and Thorn Pieces; or, The Wedded Life, Death, and Marriage of Firmian Stanislaus Siebenkaes, Parish Advocate in the Burgh of Kuhschnappel*, trans. Alexander Ewing (London: George Bell and Sons, 1892), 3906, Kindle.
2. Paul, *Flower, Fruit, and Thorn Pieces*, 3918.
3. Paul, *Flower, Fruit, and Thorn Pieces*, 3986, 3988.
4. Jean Paul, *The Campaner Thal, and Other Writings* (Boston: Ticknor and Fields, 1864), 41, Kindle.
5. Paul, *Campaner Thal*, 41.
6. Joseph Frank, "In Search of a Novel," in *Dostoevsky: A Writer in His Time* (Princeton, NJ: Princeton University Press, 2010), 549.
7. Fydor Dostoyevsky, *The Idiot*, trans. Richard Pevear and Larissa Volokhonsky (New York: Vintage, 2012), 218, Kindle.
8. Dostoyevsky, *Idiot*, 407.

Chapter 12: A Stained-Glass Reflection

1. Giles Coren, "This Lent I Will Turn Atheism to Ashes," *The Times*, March 7, 2025, www.thetimes.co.uk/article/lent-atheism-faith-anglican-religion-ntxm5xhf7.
2. Karl Barth, *Church Dogmatics*, vol. 2, part 1, ed. G. W.

Bromiley and T. F. Torrance (Edinburgh: T&T Clark, 1936–69), 187.

3. Barth, *Church Dogmatics*, 2.1, 188.
4. Karl Barth, *Church Dogmatics*, vol. 1, part 2, ed. G. W. Bromiley and T. F. Torrance (Edinburgh: T&T Clark, 1936–69), 320.
5. Barth, *Church Dogmatics* 1.2, 321.
6. Makoto Fujimura, *Art and the Theology of Making* (New Haven, CT: Yale University Press, 2020), 7, Kindle.
7. Ellen Davis, "The Preachers as Public Imaginer," lecture given at Trinity Church, Princeton, NJ, September 2018.
8. Jerry Spangler, "Like a Cloud, Beautiful Sound: The Art of John Lennon," *Deseret News*, August 31, 1997, www.deseret.com/1997/8/31/19331715/like-a-cloud-beautiful-sound-the-art-of-john-lennon/.
9. Karl Barth, *Church Dogmatics*, vol. 4, part 1, ed. G. W. Bromiley and T. F. Torrance (Edinburgh: T&T Clark, 1936–69), 480. See also Kimlyn J. Bender, "Karl Barth and the Question of Atheism," *Theology Today* 70, no. 3 (2013): 276.
10. Bender, "Karl Barth and the Question of Atheism," 275.
11. James K. A. Smith, "I'm a Philosopher. We Can't Think Our Way out of This Mess," *Christian Century*, March 10, 2021, www.christiancentury.org/article/how-my-mind-has-changed/i-m-philosopher-we-can-t-think-our-way-out-mess.

GLOSSARY

absurd, the: The fundamental struggle that arises when human beings seek meaning, order, or clarity in a universe that appears indifferent or silent.

absurdism: A philosophical view that holds that although life lacks ultimate or inherent meaning, one must go on living and may even discover freedom, defiance, and joy in that realization. Albert Camus is most closely associated with this view, developing it as a response not only to nihilism but also to existentialism, particularly as represented by Kierkegaard and Sartre.

allegory of the cave: Plato's famous parable in *The Republic*, where prisoners mistake shadows on a wall for reality. When one prisoner escapes and sees the outside world, he returns to free the others but is rejected. It's a picture of the soul's journey from ignorance to truth, and the painful resistance truth often meets.

atheism: Broadly, the absence of belief in God. In the modern world, it is less an act of rebellion against God and more a default. It is not always angry or defiant in our world but is ordinary and expected.

Barth, Karl (1886–1968): A Swiss reformed theologian who resisted Nazi ideology and liberal Protestantism. Barth is one of the most influential Protestant theologians of the twentieth century.

Bonhoeffer, Dietrich (1906–45): A German Lutheran pastor and theologian executed by the Nazis for plotting to assassinate Hitler. His writings on Christianity's role in the secular world challenged the church in his day and continue to speak into ours.

Burnham, Bo (1990–): An American comedian, filmmaker, musician, and YouTuber whose work blends humor with existential angst. Best known for satire, he created the Netflix special *Inside*, which captures his day-to-day life and deteriorating mental health in isolation.

Camus, Albert (1913–60): A French-Algerian writer and philosopher who received the Nobel Prize in Literature in 1957. Camus wrote about the absurdity of the human condition in his most well-known works, *The Stranger*, *The Plague*, and *The Myth of Sisyphus*.

closed system: The worldview that includes only what can be measured, observed, or explained from within. It leaves no room for transcendence or mystery beyond the material world. The *Humanist Manifestos* helped formalize this view.

culture wars: The ongoing clash between opposing viewpoints and visions of the good: secular versus religious, progressive versus traditional. These conflicts are not new, but they have become increasingly hostile as the shared language and space for debate continue to erode.

deconstruction: Broadly, the process of questioning, dismantling, or reinterpreting long-held beliefs, texts, or systems. The term is nuanced, with roots in philosophy and postmodernism, but today it often refers to general spiritual disorientation.

Descartes, René (1596–1650): A French philosopher, mathematician, and scientist often regarded as the founder of modern philosophy. He sought certainty through radical doubt and is famous for his statement, "I think, therefore I am" (*Cogito ergo sum*), which became the foundation of his philosophical system.

Dostoyevsky, Fyodor (1821–81): A Russian novelist and

thinker often regarded as one of the greatest novelists in world literature. His masterpieces, such as *The Brothers Karamazov*, *Demons*, and *Notes from Underground*, are known for their psychologically complex characters and deep explorations of moral struggle, suffering, and faith.

edgelord: Someone who deliberately attempts to shock or offend online, often to appear edgy or superior.

Eliot, T. S. (1888–1965): One of the most celebrated poets of the twentieth century and the 1948 winner of the Nobel Prize in Literature. He was also a literary critic, playwright, and editor who helped shape the modernist movement in poetry.

Enlightenment: An intellectual and cultural movement of the seventeenth and eighteenth centuries that emphasized reason, science, and individualism over tradition and religious authority. Also known as the Age of Reason, it reshaped Western thought, influenced political revolutions, and laid the groundwork for modern secularism.

epistemology: The theory of knowledge or how we know what we know and what counts as truth and certainty.

gallows humor: Dark, often irreverent humor that makes light of death, suffering, or other forms of tragedy and despair.

ghost at the feast: Grief, guilt, or the absence that lingers beneath modern life. The image comes from *Macbeth*, where Banquo's ghost appears at a banquet, haunting Macbeth with the truth that cannot be silenced.

Cioran, Emil (1911–95): A Romanian philosopher and essayist known for his philosophical pessimism and aphoristic style. His writings dwell on death, despair, and the silence of God, and he lived his life as a failure, on purpose.

Henley, William Ernest (1849–1903): A British poet, writer, and editor best known for his short poem "Invictus," which celebrates self-mastery and defiance in the face of suffering.

Holbein, Hans (the Younger) (1497/8–1543): A German-Swiss painter of the Northern Renaissance, renowned for his precise portraits and refined detail. Working in Basel and later at the English court of Henry VIII, he captured leading figures of the Reformation and humanism, including Erasmus and Thomas More. His art combines Renaissance realism with subtle theological and political insight.

Huxley, Aldous (1894–1963): An English writer and philosopher known for his wit and pessimistic satire. His most famous novel, *Brave New World*, highlighted his distrust of twentieth-century politics and technology.

infobesity: The state of being overwhelmed by excessive amounts of information. It describes the digital age's flood of data, noise, and distraction.

Kierkegaard, Søren (1813–55): A Danish philosopher and theologian often considered the father of existentialism. He also wrote under several pseudonyms exploring anxiety, despair, and the leap of faith required to live authentically.

man-God: The modern view of elevating human power and autonomy to divine status. It names the shift from dependence on God to self-deification.

Melville, Herman (1819–91): An American novelist and writer of the American Renaissance period. He is best known for *Moby-Dick*, a dark, sprawling novel now considered a cornerstone of modern American literature.

meh-ism: A form of passive nihilism marked by indifference and quiet surrender. Meh-ists don't rage at the world, they shrug in resignation. It reflects people too exhausted to protest, too distracted to believe, and too numb to care.

metamodernism: The cultural condition emerging beyond postmodernism. It offers a way of contextualizing the paradoxes of our time as it oscillates between modernism and postmodernism. It sees truth as complicated, yet still worth seeking. It's the tone of a generation that is skeptical, but still searching.

mood: More than an emotion, mood is defined as the atmosphere through which the world reveals itself. It shapes what we notice, how we interpret life, and what we see as real. Entire societies and ages are shaped by the mood that structures their beliefs and sense of meaning.

Nagel, Thomas (1937–): An American philosopher and professor of philosophy and law emeritus at New York University. In his essay "The Absurd," he writes that the more we know, the more meaningless life can feel.

Nietzsche, Friedrich (1844–1900): A German philosopher and cultural critic known for his radical critique of religion, moral systems, and absolute truth. He confronted the rise of nihilism in a post-Christian world, warning of the collapse of meaning that would follow the "death of God." His work shaped existentialism, postmodernism, and much of our modern culture.

nihilism: The belief that life has no inherent meaning, value, or purpose. It often emerges when belief in God collapses and there is nothing to replace it. Nihilism is not just a theory but a mood, a cultural undercurrent of our age.

nihilism (active): A defiant response to the collapse of meaning. Instead of passivity, it chooses to create value through will and protest. For Nietzsche, it was tied to the will to power. In the book, it appears in the fight to shape the world and keep on living even when truth and meaning have shattered.

nihilism (passive): The quiet surrender that follows the collapse of meaning when nothing rises to take its place. Nietzsche saw it as the soul's exhaustion and resignation to meaninglessness. In the book, it is the slow fade of apathy, numbness, and checked-out living.

nihilistic extremism: A violent form of active nihilism that seeks meaning through protest, rage, and destruction. In the book, it appears as the raze craze and toxic voidism, a form of rage that masks the despair and collapse of meaning.

November of the soul: A melancholic state marked by the slow descent into anguish, futility, and the cold weight of meaninglessness. It's the kind of mood that draws you to cemeteries, not out of grief but because their silence understands you.

numbed realism: A survival strategy in response to the absurdity and overload of modern life. It is not denial, not despair, but the quiet decision to stop feeling too much. It can be understood as a way of staying functional—or numbing—when meaning feels out of reach. It is a form of passive nihilism marked by emotional detachment and psychological drift.

Peterson, Jordan (1962–): A Canadian psychologist, author, and cultural commentator known for his critiques of postmodernism and radical progressivism. His views are loved by some and loathed by others. His work speaks to those trying to reclaim meaning in our modern age.

Plato (c. 428/427–348/347 BCE): An ancient Greek philosopher whose work laid the foundation for Western thought. He argued that truth, justice, and meaning exist in a higher, eternal realm of Forms. He saw these as realities we reach not through divine revelation but through reason.

postmodernism: A broad cultural and intellectual movement characterized by skepticism toward universal truths, objective knowledge, and fixed meanings. Arising in the late twentieth century, it questions the assumptions of modernism, such as progress, rationality, and authority and emphasizes subjectivity, plurality, and the role of power in shaping truth. Postmodernism often embraces ambiguity, irony, and fragmentation in philosophy, art, literature, and beyond.

practical polytheism: The modern habit of turning to many "gods" to satisfy our needs. These gods are not spirits or statues but things like success, pleasure, health, and image. But the irony is this: The gods we chase often harm us more than they help.

raze craze: The cultural obsession with destroying institutions, traditions, or beliefs as a form of active nihilism. It is protest without any vison for renewal but the annihilation of everything that doesn't align with one's beliefs or vision for the world. It is fueled by a craving for power in a world that feels meaningless.

Sagan, Carl (1934–96): An American astronomer and author best known for popularizing science and promoting a universe without divine presence.

Sartre, Jean Paul (1905–80): A French philosopher and novelist who received the Nobel Prize for Literature in 1964 but refused it. He is one of the key figures in the philosophy of existentialism and phenomenology.

Scientific Revolution: A period of scientific and philosophical change in the sixteenth and seventeenth centuries, during which scientific discoveries, methods, and philosophy shifted authority from tradition and divine revelation to reason and observation, redefining how people understood the world.

screw-it mode: A posture of passive nihilism marked by sarcasm and resignation. It shrugs off purpose and meaning, trading them for dark humor, cheap relief, and emotional detachment. It is a form of surrender to meaninglessness.

Shelley, Mary (1797–1851): An English novelist best known for her Gothic novel *Frankenstein*, which is widely considered to be one of the earliest examples of science fiction. It is a story that explores the consequences of science and what happens when humans try to play God.

tribalism: A deep loyalty to a group that shares a common worldview, often at the expense of others.

Tolkien, J. R. R. (1892–1973): An English writer, philologist, and Catholic who authored The Lord of the Rings trilogy and *The Hobbit*. His mythic world helped define modern fantasy, combining epic scale with deep imagination and timeless themes of good and evil.

toxic voidism: A darker outgrowth of nihilism, where people mistake rage or radicalism for meaning. It replaces reflection with reaction. In this mode, destruction is confused for purpose, and ideology becomes a substitute for transformation. It often feeds the raze craze.

troll: A figure of nihilistic mischief in the digital age. Someone who delights in outrage and disruption while hiding behind the safety of a screen. The troll is a kind of gladiator in a digital Colosseum, but someone who wants spectacle more than substance.

vibrant voidism: A posture that accepts that life has no ultimate meaning but refuses to give in to despair. Vibrant voidists build meaning through will, creativity, and protest. They do things like meme death, laugh at the absurd, and live with defiance in the face of meaninglessness.

Wallace, David Foster (1962–2008): An American novelist, essayist, and university professor of English and creative writing. His writing is known for being dense, ironic, and emotionally raw.

Watts, Alan (1915–73): A British philosopher, writer, and speaker known for interpreting Eastern philosophy for Western audiences. He challenged rigid religion and offered a more mystical approach.

zettabyte: A unit of digital measurement equal to one trillion gigabytes. The term is used symbolically to represent the overwhelming flood of information in the modern world.

SUGGESTED READING

Brave New World by Aldous Huxley. A dystopian novel imagining a future when people are controlled by pleasure, conditioning, and social engineering. Freedom and truth are sacrificed for stability.

The Brothers Karamazov by Fyodor Dostoyevsky. A passionate philosophical novel that uses a family drama to explore free will, suffering, justice, and the existence of God. It weaves philosophical debate with deep emotional and spiritual conflict.

Church Dogmatics by Karl Barth. The multivolume theological summa and magnum opus of Karl Barth. It is widely regarded as one of the most important Protestant theological works of the twentieth century.

Crime and Punishment by Fyodor Dostoyevsky. The story of a student who commits a murder and wrestles with guilt, justification, and redemption. A psychological and philosophical novel about morality.

Demons by Fyodor Dostoyevsky. A political novel depicting the rise of radical ideologies in nineteenth-century Russia. It follows a group of revolutionaries whose ideas spiral into chaos.

Ecclesiastes. One of the Ketuvim ("writings") of the Hebrew Bible that is considered part of the Wisdom Literature. It meditates on the meaning of life, time, and mortality, wrestling with futility and faith in a world where everything seems to pass away.

The Epic of Gilgamesh. One of the oldest surviving works of literature from ancient Mesopotamia, it is a collection of stories covering kingship, friendship, the search for immortality, and a great flood sent by the gods.

Frankenstein by Mary Shelley. A Gothic novel about a scientist who creates a creature in an unorthodox science experiment and then abandons it. It explores themes of ambition, responsibility, and the limits of human knowledge.

Humanist Manifestos I and II. Two twentieth-century declarations outlining a secular, human-centered worldview. They call for reason, ethics, and progress without reliance on religion.

The Idiot by Fyodor Dostoyevsky. A novel about a gentle and naïve man who enters high society and exposes its cruelty. It explores innocence, suffering, and failed redemption.

The *Iliad* by Homer. An epic poem set during the Trojan War, focusing on the rage of Achilles and the brutal cost of glory. It portrays gods and men in conflict and grief.

The Joyous Science by Friedrich Nietzsche. A book of aphorisms and essays on art, knowledge, and life. It includes Nietzsche's first declaration of the "death of God."

Letters and Papers from Prison by Dietrich Bonhoeffer. A collection of theological and personal writings from Bonhoeffer's final years. It reflects on Christian faith, ethics, and resistance under Nazism.

The Lord of the Rings trilogy by J. R. R. Tolkien. An epic fantasy adventure about the struggle to destroy a powerful ring that threatens all life. It blends myth, moral conflict, and heroic friendship.

Meditations on First Philosophy by René Descartes. A foundational philosophical treatise that uses doubt to seek certainty, arguing for the existence of God and the immortality of the soul. It introduces the famous statement "I think, therefore I am."

Moby-Dick by Herman Melville. An American novel about a whaling voyage and one man's obsessive pursuit of a white whale. It combines sea adventure, metaphysical inquiry, and tragedy.

Nausea by Jean-Paul Sartre. A philosophical novel about a man who begins to feel the absurd weight of existence. It introduces Sartre's existentialist ideas through fiction.

Notes from Underground by Fyodor Dostoyevsky. A dark monologue by a bitter man alienated from society and himself. A foundational work of existential literature.

The *Odyssey* by Homer. The story of Odysseus' long journey home after the Trojan War. It follows themes of identity, hospitality, perseverance, and reconciliation.

The Plague by Albert Camus. A novel about a town quarantined by an outbreak of plague. It explores human suffering, solidarity, and the struggle for moral action in absurd conditions.

The Republic by Plato. A Socratic dialogue that explores justice, education, and the ideal state. It includes the allegory of the cave and the theory of the Forms.

The Stranger by Albert Camus. A novel that explores existentialism and the absurdity of life through the story of Meursault, who kills an unnamed man without a clear motive and faces trial.

Thus Spoke Zarathustra by Friedrich Nietzsche. A philosophical novel that presents the overman, the death of God, eternal recurrence, and the will to power. It is written in a prophetic and poetic style.

The Trouble with Being Born by Emil Cioran. A book of bleak, poetic aphorisms on time, death, and the painful nature of consciousness. Cioran meditates on the burden of existence with ironic clarity.

The Will to Power by Friedrich Nietzsche. A posthumous collection of notes exploring power, morality, and the revaluation of values. It outlines Nietzsche's later philosophical concerns.